Beryl Favell.
July 78.

A FIELD GUIDE TO THE
# Orchids
of Britain and Europe

A FIELD GUIDE TO THE

# Orchids

of Britain and Europe
with North Africa and the Middle East

JOHN G WILLIAMS     ANDREW E WILLIAMS
NORMAN ARLOTT

*with illustrations in colour of 245 species, subspecies and varieties, by*
*Norman Arlott*

Foreword by Roger Tory Peterson

COLLINS
St. James's Place, London

For Daphne M. Ball
in esteem, gratitude and friendship

First published in Great Britain by William Collins, Sons & Co., Ltd 1978

Designed and produced by London Editions Ltd,
30 Uxbridge Road, London W12 8ND

ISBN 0 00 219314 0

Printed and bound in Yugoslavia by
Mladinska knjiga, Ljubljana

# CONTENTS

# FOREWORD by Roger Tory Peterson

It comes as a surprise to many of us to learn that Orchidaceae is the second largest family of plants in the vegetable kingdom, numbering between 15,000 and 35,000 species, depending on which authority is consulted. Yet the species are by no means commonplace. They enjoy a mystique that transcends that of any other family of wild flowers. Their rainbow colours, bizarre shapes and patterns beguile the eye. Their curious adaptations to life forces and the environment intrigue the imagination.

Most people think of orchids mainly in terms of cattleyas, cymbidiums and other flamboyant blooms of the florists' trade; they are unaware that some species are so small and modest that they may escape the notice of all but the most sharp-eyed botanist. Orchids are to be found on every continent except Antarctica. Absent only from the polar regions, they have adapted to almost every environment, from hot, moist jungles to parched deserts and cool tundra, and from sea-level to altitudes above timberline in the higher mountains.

A great many tropical orchids are epiphytic, anchoring themselves to the rough trunks and outstretched limbs of forest trees where they take much of their nourishment from the humid air. Those in temperate zones, such as the ones dealt with in this book, which covers Europe and the Mediterranean basin are terrestrial.

An orchid may scatter as many as two or three million seeds, so minute as to be like dust in the wind' To germinate and grow, the infant plant must somehow form an intimate partnership with fungi in and around its roots, enabling it to take food from decaying material in the soil. For two to four years a terrestrial orchid may remain as a leafless underground shoot before it sees the light of day. Some species such as the twayblades may take another ten years before they flower.

Although a few species are structurally adapted to pollinate themselves, most orchids rely on their seductively coloured lips to lure insects to perform the rites of pollination. Some, such as the bee-orchids, *Ophrys*, and certain tropical orchids have lips that mimic bees or wasps and scents that stimulate males of these insects to attempt sexual union with them. During this pseudo-copulation pollen is transferred to the stigma of the plant and the reproductive cycle is triggered. The variations on this theme are many. In most orchids, however, the attraction of the flowers to insects is in terms of food, not sex. But one ponders the evolutionary processes that have made pollination so complicated or specialized. An extreme example is an orchid in Madagascar that has such a long nectar spur that it can be probed and fertilized only by a single species of insect, a sphinx moth with a tongue more than twelve inches long.

These peculiar adaptations interested Charles Darwin who had already come to grips with the origin of species through natural selection. In 1862 he published a book on *The Various Contrivances by which Orchids are Fertilized by Insects*, a work that was reissued in 1877 with many additional details.

A conservation note about these vulnerable plants is in order. There is no longer need to collect and press specimens of orchids for the sole purpose of substantiating records, either in Europe or in North America. A good colour transparency of the living plant is really much more satisfactory; it takes up less room and gives more lasting pleasure. Such photographs can be taken *in situ*, using either available light or controlled flash. In today's world few orchids can afford the attrition imposed by the vasculum and the plant press. They should be looked at long and appreciatively, perhaps photographed, and then left where they are growing.

John Williams, the senior author of this book, might be described as one of those rarities, a true naturalist of the old school. He is not solely an ornithologist, a lepidopterist or a botanist, but rather the sum of all these and much more. He is aware of the total environment and knows intimately its various components. His son Andrew has followed in his footsteps. As junior author of this guide he has augmented the material collected over the years by his father.

In looking over the fine illustrations by Norman Arlott I am reminded of rare summer days in the south of Spain, islands in the Baltic, woodlands in Crete, moors in Scotland and other magic places where I found orchids new to me and where a Field Guide such as this would have given me names.

_Roger T. Peterson_

# INTRODUCTION

There can be little doubt that of all European wild flowers few species can rival the indigenous orchids in beauty and variety of form and colour. These attributes, coupled with the adventurous journeys one must undertake in searching for some of the rarer species, have endowed orchids with a special glamour all their own. Often some rare and lovely species has its particular habitat in a region of great natural beauty, remote and difficult of access but infinitely rewarding. The pursuit of such gems is in truth a treasure hunt.

Anyone who embarks on an orchid odyssey will build up a wealth of unforgettable memories. I can well recall my own feelings of awe and delight on finding my first Calypso Orchids, flowering in the dank moss and pine-needle litter of a far northern forest; and amongst the temples of ancient Greece—to which I paid little heed—the unbelievable beauty of my first Mirror Orchids. Even wading in ice-cold sphagnum bogs for the tiny, elusive Bog Orchid has had its pleasures. And there must be many who have experienced similar delights.

Yet, strangely, in spite of the popular interest taken in this family of plants, there has been no adequately illustrated and comprehensive book published on them. It is to fill this gap that the present book has been written.

The idea for such a book was first conceived many years ago, when wartime service in the Royal Air Force took me to many orchid-rich localities in the Middle East and various Mediterranean countries. It was then that I began to build up a collection of drawings and colour sketches of the orchids I found. In later years this was augmented by material collected by my son Andrew, co-author of this book. I am indebted to artist Norman Arlott who has turned these original sketches into botanical paintings of great beauty and accuracy.

It is my pleasure to record my gratitude to the many persons who have helped me. I would mention especially Professor Ake Holm and his colleagues at the Zoological Institute, Uppsala, Sweden; Drs Roger M. Polhill and Granville Lucas of the Kew Herbarium; Dr Bertil Kullenberg, Bengt Jacobsson and Rudi Jelinek of Sweden; Dr Dieter Kock of the Natur-Museum Senckenberg, Germany; Dr J. B. Gillett of the East African Herbarium; Dr A. C. van Bruggen of Leiden University and Dr Stella Rogers of the University of London; Dr Kjell Gustafsson of Sweden; and I am particularly indebted to Mr Jeffrey Wood, for his painstaking checking of the plates and nomenclature, and to his colleagues Mr Peter Taylor and Dr Phillip Cribb, all of the Royal Botanic Gardens, Kew. I would also thank Mrs Daphne M. Ball, Mrs Morna Hale, Mr Richard Daniel, Mr Basil Parsons, Mr Eric Hosking, Mr Robert Gillmor, Mrs W. D. Just and Mr and and Mrs Edward Frewin who all assisted in various ways. I am also grateful to my publishers London Editions Ltd, and in particular to Mr Hugh Begg and Mr Robin Wright for their helpful advice, enthusiasm and courtesy. I must also pay tribute to my R.A.F. colleagues of earlier days for their tolerance of my idiosyncrasies with birds, bugs and botany, albeit with sometimes ribald comment!

## The Recognition of an Orchid

Orchids belong to the great group of flowering plants termed Monocotyledons, those plants which on germination of the seed possess only one embryo leaf (cotyledon) as opposed to the two which appear in seedlings of the other division, the Dicotyledons. Members of the Monocotyledon group include the orchids, lilies, amaryllids, irises and related families.

An orchid flower may be recognized by the number and arrangement of its perianth segments—the three similar outer segments called *sepals*, and the three inner called *petals*. The median petal, known as the lip or *labellum*, is often larger than the two lateral petals and is modified in structure and more brightly coloured. In many orchids there is a hollow, nectar-producing *spur* at the base of the *labellum*. Projecting from the centre of the orchid flower is a thickened structure known as the *column*, combining the male and female organs of reproduction. At or near the top of the column are the *anthers*, the male section of the organ containing the pollen grains. These are grouped in masses, normally two to four, called *pollinia*. Below the anthers is the upper female portion of the column, the *stigma*, a depressed and often sticky surface to which the pollen grains adhere during pollination. In many orchids, interposed between the anthers and the stigma, is a structure called the *rostellum*. Evolved from an infertile stigma, this serves to inhibit self-fertilization, by preventing the pollen grains reaching the stigma of the same flower. Below the stigma, beneath the perianth, is the *ovary*, containing myriads of tiny ovules, which after fertilization develop into vast numbers of extremely small seeds. The ovary itself expands into an egg-shaped or cylindrical capsule.

The possession of a column and the modified median petal, the lip, distinguish an orchid from all other flowers. An additional character, shared with many other Monocotyledons, is that the leaf veins in orchids are parallel.

## Reproduction

Orchids have two main methods of maintaining their numbers—by vegetative multiplication from tubers and root buds, and by production of seeds. There is also a third method: in the case of the tiny Bog Orchid (*Hammarbya*) small projections known as bulbils grow at the tips of the leaves and break off to form new plants.

Most orchids rely upon insects, especially members of the Hymenoptera and Lepidoptera, to help the fertilization of their flowers. When an insect in search of nectar visits an orchid flower it comes in contact with the viscidium, a sticky disc connected by a stalk to the pollinia. The viscidium adheres to the insect, taking with it the pollinia which are carried on to another flower so ensuring cross-fertilization.

A few orchids, notably some of the genus *Epipactis*, are routinely self-pollinated, the projecting pollinia fragmenting so that pollen grains reach the stigma. Self-pollination can occur in various other orchids, including some members of the genus *Ophrys*, normally pollinated by insects. Where a flower has not been visited by the normal insect pollinator, the pollinia stalks shrink, as the flower withers, pulling the pollen masses away from the anthers to hange forwards above the stigma. Wind movement is then sufficient to bring the pollen into contact with the stigma, and self-fertilization is achieved.

## Region Covered

This book describes and illustrates all the species and many of the subspecies and varieties of orchids found in Europe east to the Urals and Caucasus and inclusive of Iceland and the Faeroes, the Middle Eastern countries bordering or adjacent to the Mediterranean, the Mediterranean islands, North Africa and the Atlantic islands of Madeira, the Azores and the Canaries.

## How to Use the Book

A simplified key to the orchid genera will enable the user of this book to narrow his identification to genus, after which a perusal of the text and illustrations will enable a name to be given to most orchid specimens. There are additional artificial keys to the species of the large genera *Orchis* and *Ophrys*. However, there will be times, especially in the case of such very variable species as the Marsh Orchids (*Dactylorhiza*), which also hybridize readily, when an individual plant will defy classification except by a botanist specializing in that particular genus: and even then an identification may be controversial between different experts!

In the interests of conservation it cannot be too strongly stressed that this book should be used *in the field* to identify any given specimen. Do not pick or dig up the orchid you have found to identify it at home. If you want a record of its appearance use a camera. Remember that the future of many of our rarer orchids is very precarious, especially in western Europe. Habitats continue to be built over or otherwise utilized, bogs and marshes drained and woodland areas cut down. Please do not increase their rarity by thoughtless picking or removal.

## Nomenclature and Taxonomy

The nomenclature and taxonomy followed in this book in the main adhere to the guidelines laid down in vol. 5 of *Flora Europaea*. It is more than likely that the future will see further revisions and changes affecting some of the 'difficult' species in groups such as *Ophrys* and *Dactylorhiza*, and an upgrading to specific status of some orchid populations now classified as subspecies. However this is more the concern of the professional taxonomist than of the amateur naturalist, whose main pleasure will be in searching for, finding and appreciating flowers of such rare beauty. I wish you good hunting.

## John G. Williams

# HOW TO USE THE ARTIFICIAL KEYS

Artificial keys to genera and species are not foolproof, especially with families such as Orchidaceae, where there is considerable blurring between species and hybridization, making exact identification often extremely difficult, even for the expert. There is also dispute among taxonomists over the divisions between and nomenclature of genera and species. That being said, the following keys, for guiding the reader to the correct genus and, in the case of the genera *Ophrys* and *Orchis*, to the species, should prove a help in tracking down the plant in the field. The possession of a magnifying glass is often essential, since many of the features used in identification are very small. I would also point out that the beginner may find the keys harder to follow than the species descriptions in the main part of the book since they presuppose some botanical knowledge on the part of the user.

Briefly, the keys act as a filter. Starting at 1 on each key, the user makes up his mind which of usually two possible alternative descriptions his specimen most resembles, and then proceeds to that part of the key indicated by the numeral on the right. By this process of elimination he should arrive at a genus or species which he can then check in the texts and illustrations.

# ARTIFICIAL KEY TO THE GENERA

I   Orchids lacking chlorophyll or green leaves                                    2
    Orchids with chlorophyll, green leaves or green bract-like scales on a
    green stem                                                                     5

2   Spur long or relatively long                                                   3
    Spur very short or absent                                                      4

3   Lip entire, pointing downwards                    *Limodorum* (p. 146)
    Lip three-lobed, pointing upwards                 *Epipogium* (p. 146)

4   Flowers pale brown; stem with numerous brown scales  *Neottia* (p. 140)
    Flowers whitish or yellowish; stem with two to four long sheathing scales
                                                      *Corallorhiza* (p. 134)

5   Flowers lacking a spur                                                         6
    Flowers possessing a spur                                                      20

6   Flowers medium-sized or large with inflated slipper-shaped lip                 7
    Lip not inflated or slipper-shaped                                             8

7   Stem bearing one leaf; anther one; tuber solitary     *Calypso* (p. 134)
    Stem bearing two to four leaves; anthers two; rhizomatous
                                                      *Cypripedium* (p. 26)

8   Flowers medium-sized with enlarged glabrous or hairy lip resembling
    the body of an insect or spider; central area of lip, the speculum, often
    distinctively coloured                      *Ophrys* (see pp. 17-20)
    Flowers small or medium-sized; lip glabrous without speculum and not
    insect-like                                                                    9

9   Lip pointing upwards                                                           10
    Lip pointing downwards                                                         12

10  Plant very small with lip shorter than sepals; petals about half length of
        sepals                                        *Hammarbya* (p. 137)
    Plant small with lip about as long as sepals; petals about same length as
        sepals                                                                     11

11  Sepals short, more than 3mm; single leaf borne above pseudobulb
                                                      *Malaxis* (p. 136)
    Sepals at least 5mm; plant with two pseudobulbs growing alongside one
        another and joined by a short stolon          *Liparis* (p. 134)

12  Lip divided into two distinct sections by constriction of middle, a concave
        basal part, the hypochile, and a downward or forward pointing distal
        part, the epichile                                                         13
    Lip not so divided                                                             15

13   Hypochile with erect lateral lobes on each side; epichile distinctly
       pendent, tongue-like                              *Serapias* (pp. 60-76)
       Hypochile without marked lateral lobes and epichile not distinctly
       pendent                                                              14

14   Flowers erect or sub-erect, sessile or with only very short stalks, in more
       or less one-sided spike           *Cephalanthera* (part) (pp. 144-56)
       Flowers held horizontally or pendent, pedunculate; column short
                                                        *Epipactis* (pp. 148-55)

15   Flowers arranged in one to three spiral rows or in a one-sided spike;
       flowers usually white                                              16
       Flowers not arranged in spiral rows; flowers variously coloured, yellowish,
       greenish or mauve                                                  17

16   Leaves with parallel veins, not net-veined; lip equal to sepals in length
                                                        *Spiranthes* (p. 133)
       Leaves often conspicuously net-veined; lip shorter than sepals
                                                        *Goodyera* (p. 136)

17   Plant small; leaves slender and grass-like, equalling or longer than stem;
       lip entire or slightly lobed                 *Chamorchis* (p. 122)
       Leaves usually shorter than stem, oblong to linear-lanceolate; lip deeply
       lobed                                                              18

18   Leaves numerous; lip shaped like a man with long lateral and medial
       lobes                                            *Aceras* (p. 66)
       Stem with two bract-like or ovate leaves; lip not man-shaped      19

19   Lip strongly three-lobed                        *Herminium* (p. 132)
       Lip deeply two-lobed; two broadly oval leaves on stem   *Listera* (p. 140)

20   Flowers with a spur                                                 21

21   Lip divided into two sections by constriction of middle, a concave basal
       part, the hypochile, and a distal part, the epichile
                                               *Cephalanthera* (part) (pp. 144-56)

       Lip not so divided                                                22

22   Spur very short, not more than 2mm              *Nigritella* (p. 122)
       Spur at least 5mm                                                 23

23  Lip with median lobe exceeding lateral lobes and spirally twisted; sepals
    and petals converging to form a helmet; bracts equal to or shorter than
    flowers                    *Himantoglossum* (p. 68-78)
    Median lobe of lip not spirally twisted; sepals spreading            24

24  Plant extremely robust; lateral sepals spreading; median lobe of lip
    variable, a little longer or shorter than laterals, but not spirally twisted;
    bracts longer than flowers              *Barlia* (p. 78)
    Plants not outstandingly robust                      25

25  Lip strap-like                               26
    Lip not strap-like                            28

26  Lip entire; flowers greenish-white      *Platanthera* (pp. 128-30)
    Lip lobed                                 27

27  Lip divided into three strap-like lobes; flowers green; endemic to Canary
    Islands                         *Habenaria* (p. 132)
    Lip strap-like, three-lobed at apex, the laterals parallel, longer than
    median lobe                    *Coeloglossum* (p. 126)

28  Lip with lobes prolonged into long thread-like processes
                                    *Comperia* (p. 106)
    Lip without long thread-like processes                  29

29  Inflorescence strongly globose; perianth segments with spatulate tips;
    flowers pinkish-lilac                *Traunsteinera* (p. 122)
    Inflorescence not strongly globose; perianth segments without spatulate
    tips                                    30

30  Two heart-shaped leaves on stem; flowers yellowish-green
                                    *Gennaria* (p. 132)
    Without two heart-shaped leaves on stem                  31

31  Lip more or less converged with other perianth segments so that flower
    appears subcampanulate              *Leucorchis* (p. 126)
    Lip and perianth segments not so converged               32

32  Dorsal and lateral sepals fused almost to apex; flowers greenish; stem
    with single basal leaf and two foliaceous sheaths above
                                    *Steveniella* (p. 106)
    Dorsal and lateral sepals not fused                     33

33  Lateral sepals and petals fused at base; sepals short, not more than 4mm
                                    *Neotinea* (p. 80)
    Lateral sepals and petals not fused                     34

34   Flowers in more or less one-sided spike; bursicle absent
                                            *Neottianthe* (p. 126)
        Flowers not arranged in a one-sided spike                35

35   At least some perianth segments converging to form a hood; lip three-
        lobed; spur very long and slender, at least 11mm          36
        Perianth segments either converging or spreading; lip variable, entire,
        lobed or three-dentate at apex; spur usually not very slender, at least
        5mm                                                       37

36   Lip deeply three-lobed with two longitudinal ridges at base
                                            *Anacamptis* (p. 80)
        Lip shallowly three-lobed, without ridges at base   *Gymnadenia* (p. 124)

37   Floral bracts membranous; tubers entire        *Orchis* (see pp. 29-31)
        At least lower floral bracts leaf-like; tubers palmately lobed
                                            *Dactylorhiza* (pp. 110-20)

# KEY TO THE GENUS OPHRYS L.

1    Connective structure between anthers blunt ended                      2
     Connective structure between anthers with pointed tip                 8

2    Inner perianth segments white, yellowish or green                     3
     Inner perianth segments purplish or reddish, at least at base         5

3    Lip with flat margin; marginal zone yellow, glabrous or hairy
                                                    *O. lutea* (p. 56)
     Lip with more or less deflexed margin; marginal zone velvety, may be
        yellow; inner perianth segments green                             4

4    Inner perianth segments white to whitish-green; lip 7-9mm
                                                    *O. pallida* (p. 58)
     Inner perianth segments green; lip 13-23mm; side lobes shorter than
        central lobe                                *O. fusca* (p. 54)

5    Lip deeply three-lobed; lateral lobes velvety and deflexed so that lip
        appears spherical and inflated         *O. bombylifera* (p. 46)
     Lip entire to deeply three-lobed; lateral lobes not velvety or deflexed  6

6    Outer perianth segments purplish; lip entire, rarely shallowly three-lobed
                                               *O. tenthredinifera* (p. 42)
     Outer perianth segments green or yellowish; lip distinctly three-lobed   7

7    Inner perianth segments very slender, velvety; middle lobe of lip entire
        or two-lobed; speculum small, pale violet-blue   *O. insectifera* (p. 58)
     Inner perianth segments ovate to lanceolate, hairy; middle lobe of lip
        entire or slightly emarginate; speculum large, bright blue with yellow
        margin                                     *O. speculum* (p. 58)

8    Lateral lobes of lip with basal protuberances; speculum usually with a
        whitish or yellowish margin                                       9
     Lateral lobes of lip without basal protuberances; speculum with or
        without pale margin                                              21

9    Outer perianth segments green; lip with or without an appendage     10
     Outer perianth segments pink or purplish; lip usually with an appendage  16

10   Lip entire                                                           11
     Lip three-lobed                                                      12

11 Speculum without a coloured margin, usually H-shaped; inner perianth
      segments at least half length of outer perianth segments
                                          *O. sphegodes* (part) (pp. 48-50)
    Speculum with a white, yellow or greenish margin, variable, H-shaped or
      shield-shaped; inner perianth segments one fifth to one third length of
      outer perianth segments            *O. fuciflora* (part) (pp. 38-42)

12 Lateral lobes of lip glabrous; speculum usually H-shaped              13
    Lateral lobes of lip hairy; speculum variable, H-shaped, shield-shaped or
      composed of small spots                                          14

13 Speculum without pale margin; lip 5-15(-17)mm
                                          *O. sphegodes* (part) (pp. 48-50)
    Speculum often with white margin; lip 10-13(-15)mm
                                          *O. spruneri* (part) (p.52)

14 Lip blackish-purple; speculum H-shaped, shield-shaped or small spots,
      white or bluish, with white margin                              15
    Lip brown; speculum shield-shaped, blue or dark violet with yellow margin
                                          *O. carmelii* (p. 34)

15 Lip with lateral lobes spreading           *O. cretica* (part) (p. 30)
    Lip with lateral lobes strongly reflexed      *O. kotschyi* (p. 30)

16 Inner perianth segments two-thirds length of outer perianth segments;
      speculum half moon-shaped without a coloured margin
                                          *O. lunulata* (part) (p. 34)
    Inner perianth segments up to half length of outer perianth segments;
      speculum variable but not half moon-shaped, with a whitish or yellow
      margin                                                          17

17 Lip entire or subentire                                            18
    Lip three-lobed                                                   19

18 Basal protuberances of lip up to 3mm; appendage of lip large, three dentate
                                          *O. fuciflora* (part) (pp. 38-42)
    Basal protuberances of lip short and inconspicuous; lip appendage small
                                          *O. arachnitiformis* (p. 54)

19 Outer perianth segments normally 10-15mm; lip appendage long or
      absent; margin of speculum yellow       *O. apifera* (p. 44)
    Outer perianth segments normally 8-10(-12)mm; lip appendage short;
      margin of speculum yellow or white                              20

20    Inner perianth segments half length of outer perianth segments; lip with
small basal protuberances; margin of speculum white
*O. cretica* (part) (p. 30)
Inner perianth segments one fifth to one half length of outer perianth
segments; lip with large or long horn-shaped basal protuberances;
margin of speculum whitish or yellow    *O. scolopax* (pp. 34-6)

| | |
|---|---|
| 21    Lip entire | 22 |
| Lip three-lobed | 27 |
| | |
| 22    Outer perianth segments green | 23 |
| Outer perianth segments pinkish or purplish | 25 |
| | |
| 23    Speculum with whitish, greenish or yellow margin | 26 |
| Speculum without a coloured margin | 24 |

24    Lip 5-15(-17)mm; without appendage; speculum usually H-shaped
*O. sphegodes* (part) (pp. 48-50)
Lip 10-12mm, with appendage; speculum usually horseshoe-shaped
*O. ferrum-equinum* (part) (p. 46)

25    Speculum usually horseshoe-shaped; lip velvety, not curved upwards
anteriorly    *O. ferrum-equinum* (part) (p. 46)
Speculum usually scutelliform; lip velvety, curved upwards anteriorly
*O. bertolonii* (p. 46)

26    Inner perianth segments at least half as long as outer perianth segments;
lip roundish to ovate in outline    *O. argolica* (part) (p. 32)
Inner perianth segments one fifth to one third length of outer perianth
segments; lip broadly obovate to almost square
*O. fuciflora* (part) (pp. 38-42)

27    Inner perianth segments at least two-thirds length of outer perianth
segments; speculum crescentic; outer perianth segments pinkish-violet
*O. lunulata* (part) (p. 34)
Inner perianth segments about half length of outer perianth segments
or shorter    28

28    Inner perianth segments about half length of outer perianth segments;
speculum variable but not crescentic; outer perianth segments green,
pinkish or purplish    29
Inner perianth segments much shorter, 2mm or less    34

29    Speculum usually horseshoe-shaped; inner perianth segments glabrous
*O. ferrum-equinum* (part) (p. 46)
Speculum variable but if horseshoe-shaped then inner perianth segments
velvety    30

30   Speculum of two thick, comma-shaped lines or two spots
                                            *O. reinholdii* (p. 32)
     Speculum not as above                                          31

31   Speculum lengthened H-shaped; lateral outer perianth segments very
        large, down-pointing                        *O. kurdica* (30)
     Speculum H-shaped or shield shaped, or of one or two lines or spots;
        lateral outer perianth segments not very large               32

32   Outer perianth segments pinkish-violet or purple; inner perianth seg-
        ments velvety; speculum with white margin   *O. argolica* (part) (p. 32)
     Outer perianth segments green or greenish-purple; inner perianth seg-
        ments glabrous or hairy; speculum with or without white margin    33

33   Lip 5-15(-17)mm, usually entire; speculum without white margin
                                            *O. sphegodes* (part) (pp. 48-50)
     Lip 10-13(-15)mm, three-lobed; speculum with white margin
                                            *O. spruneri* (part) (p. 52)

34   Side lobes of lip small            *O. fuciflora* ssp. *bornmuelleri* (p. 42)
     Side lobes of lip very large, directed upwards     *O. luristanica* (p. 34)

# KEY TO THE GENUS ORCHIS L.

1   All five perianth segments convergent to form a hood                                    2
    Lateral outer perianth segments spreading or reflexed; middle segment
        convergent into hood with two inner perianth segments                              16

2   Lip entire                                            *O. papilionacea* (p. 94)
    Lip three-lobed                                                                          3

3   Spur horizontal or curved slightly upwards; lip about as wide as or slightly
        wider than long                                                                      4
    Spur directed downwards; lip longer than wide                                            6

4   Spur very slender; flowers at apex of spike opening first     *O. boryi* (p. 98)
    Spur cylindrical; flowers at base of spike opening first                                 5

5   Spur as long as or slightly longer than lip                 *O. morio* (p. 92)
    Spur much longer than lip                              *O. longicornu* (p. 94)

6   Central lobe of lip entire or toothed; without purple spots                              7
    Central lobe of lip deeply emarginate; usually with purple spots                         8

7   Stem with 4-7 leaves; leaves linear to narrowly lanceolate; spur conical,
        incurved slightly at apex                           *O. coriophora* (p. 82)
    Stem with sheathing leaves; spur incurved, attenuated towards apex
                                                              *O. sancta* (p. 82)

8   Bracts slightly shorter than or as long as ovary; central lobe of lip not
        ending abruptly in a sharp point between the lobules                                 9
    Bracts much shorter than ovary; central lobe of lip with a sharp pointed
        tooth or teeth, or divided into long slender segments between the lobules           11

9   Outer perianth segments 3-3·5mm; spike ovoid to cylindrical; spur a
        quarter to half as long as ovary                    *O. ustulata* (p. 84)
    Outer perianth segments 6-12mm; spike conical to ovoid; spur at least
        half length of ovary                                                                10

10  Stem 15-45cm; flowers pale mauve; central lobe of lip wedge-shaped,
        notched; spur half as long as ovary                *O. tridentata* (p. 84)
    Stem 7-20cm; flowers white or greenish-pink; central lobe of lip curved,
        usually not toothed; spur as long as or longer than ovary
                                                              *O. lactea* (p. 84)

11  Lobules of middle lobe of lip long and slender                                          12
    Lobules of middle lobe of lip ovate or oblong with a central tooth                      13

12   Base of lip with two triangular ridges, scarcely papillose; lateral lobes and
       lobules of central lobe of lip more or less flat, acute    *O. italica* (p. 90)
     Base of lip without ridges, minutely papillose; lateral lobes and lobules of
       central lobe of lip obtuse                                 *O. simia* (p. 90)

13   Perianth segments brownish-purple                  *O. purpurea* (p. 88)
     Perianth segments pink or yellowish-green                              14

14   Spur narrowly cylindrical, half length of ovary; hood whitish or dull pink;
       lip pink                                           *O. militaris* (p. 88)
     Spur broadly cylindrical, a quarter to half length of ovary; hood and lip
       yellowish-green                                                     15

15   Flower spike opening from bottom           *O. punctulata* (p. 86)
     Flower spike opening from apex               *O. galilaea* (p. 86)

16   Endemic to Canary Islands; lip three-lobed; flowers pink or pink with
       red spots                                     *O. canariensis* (p. 98)
     Not endemic to Canary Islands                                         17

17   Leaves linear or lanceolate, narrowed towards tip, spreading; bracts 3-7
       veined                                            *O. laxiflora* (p. 104)
     Leaves oblong to oblong-lanceolate or oblong-ovate, rarely lanceolate;
       appressed or in basal rosette; bracts normally 1-3 veined            18

18   Spur thread-like or linear-conical, attenuate towards tip                19
     Spur cylindrical or saccate                                            20

19   Spur slender, linear-conical, wider towards the mouth
                                                        *O. anatolica* (p. 98)
     Spur thread-like, not wider towards the mouth
                                                   *O. quadripunctata* (p. 98)

20   Two lateral outer perianth segments erect or spreading; spur pointing
       downwards; bracts 5-7 veined                                        21
     Two lateral outer perianth segments deflexed, rarely erect or spreading;
       spur not pointing downwards; bracts 1-3 veined                      23

21   Lip undivided                                       *O. saccata* (p. 96)
     Lip three-lobed                                                       22

22   Flower spike long-cylindrical; spur saccate; base of lip with two incon-
       spicuous ridges                                   *O. patens* (p. 96)
     Flower spike ovoid or short-cylindrical; spur conical-cylindrical; base of
       lip with two conspicuous ridges                   *O. spitzelii* (p. 96)

23  Flowers pink to purple; outer perianth segments ovate to oblong-
      lanceolate, obtuse to acuminate          *O. mascula* (p. 100)
    Flowers pale yellow; outer perianth segments ovate-oblong, obtuse          24

24  Spur slightly shorter than ovary; flower spike dense; leaves oblong, spread
      along lower half of stem          *O. pallens* (p. 102)
    Spur as long as or longer than ovary; leaves lanceolate or oblong-
      lanceolate, crowded at base of stem          *O. provincialis* (p. 102)

# SPECIES DESCRIPTIONS AND PLATES

## Lady's Slippers *Cypripedium*

Perennials, 15-60cm. Root system a creeping rhizome; no tubers. Leaves few, normally broadly elliptic or oval; bracts leaf-like; flowers large and showy, typically one, rarely two or three per stem. Perianth composed of four spreading segments (the two lateral sepals are fused and point downwards) and a large pouch-shaped lip, inflated, bearing a resemblance to a slipper; no spur. Column stout, projects forwards and slightly downwards, partially closing lip aperture; two fertile anthers, one on each side of the column; column covered by a staminode.

The genus *Cypripedium* contains about 20 species distributed in the temperate and cold regions of Europe, Asia and North America. Others occur in subtropical areas. Countries richest in *Cypripedium* species are North America, China and Japan. In Europe only three species are found, two of which are confined to Russian localities.

**Lady's Slipper** *Cypripedium calceolus* L.
French *Sabot de Vénus* German *Frauenschuh* Italian *Forfallone*
15-50cm. Leaves three to four, broadly elliptic with conspicuous veining. Flowers solitary to two or more, large and striking; perianth segments maroon-red, contrasting with inflated yellow lip; staminode whitish with or without crimson speckles; lateral sepals fused and pointing donwards; ovary slightly hairy. An uncommon colour form, var. *flavum* Rion, has the sepals and petals pale yellow, not maroon. The Rosy Lady's Slipper *(C. macranthum)* differs in having a reddish lip; the smaller-flowered Spotted Lady's Slipper *(C. guttatum)* has a white lip with purple spots or blotches.

Occurs in northern and central Europe, westwards to Norway and the south-western Alps, eastwards through Russia to Siberia. In the British Isles now nearly extinct but still persistent in the West Riding of Yorkshire. Grows in shady deciduous and mixed woodlands, scrub, thickets and glades, often in mountainous districts and up to 1700 metres in the Tyrol; occurs usually on calcareous soils. Flowers May to July, the season varying with altitude and climate.

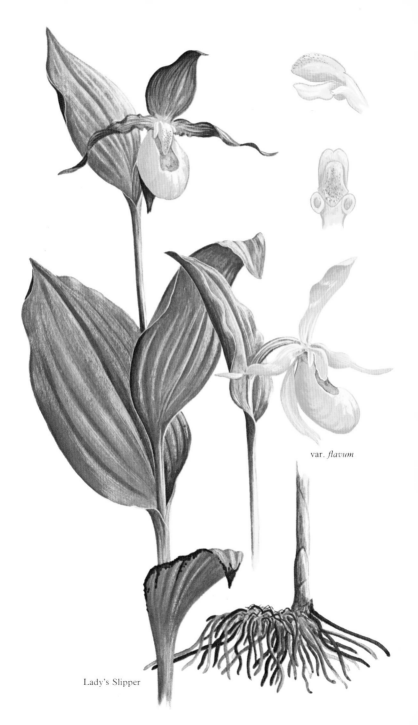

var. *flavum*

Lady's Slipper

**Rosy Lady's Slipper** *Cypripedium macranthum* Swartz
25-45cm. Leaves three to four, alternate, broadly oval and acuminate with veining. Flowers normally solitary; perianth lilac to reddish-violet; dorsal sepal broadly oval; lateral sepals united and pointed downwards; lip inflated with a narrow orifice, violet to reddish-purple; staminode whitish, speckled with violet. In var. *ventricosum* Swartz, the petals are longer than the lip and the dorsal sepal is narrower; flower colour often paler. The rosy lip distinguishes this species from *C. calceolus* and *C. guttatum*.
Frequent in central Russia from eastern White Russia to the Urals and extending eastwards to eastern Siberia. Grows in shady birch woods, forest glades and less frequently in pine forests. Often found growing alongside *C. guttatum*. Flowers June and July.

var. *ventricosum*

Rosy Lady's Slipper

**Spotted Lady's Slipper** *Cypripedium guttatum* Swartz
15-30cm, lightly pubescent. Stem slender with two ovate leaves; bract large and leaf-like. Flowers solitary, white with purplish spots or blotches; dorsal sepal broadly ovate, abruptly acute and deeply concave, spotted inside with purplish-violet; lateral sepals united almost to apex, down-pointing, greenish-white. Petals spreading, wide at base, white with purplish spots; lip strongly inflated with a broad orifice, also white with purple markings. A white variety lacking purple markings has been named var. *redowskii* Rchb. The purple spotted white flowers distinguish *C. guttatum* from the other two species.
Central Russia to *ca* 60°N, eastwards to eastern Siberia, Manchuria and Korea. Habitat includes coniferous and mixed woodland, shady glades and birch thickets. Flowers May and June.

Spotted Lady's Slipper

# Bee Orchids *Ophrys*

Perennials, 10-45(70)cm. Root system, two rounded or oval tubers. Leaves four or more usually in a rosette around base of stem, broadly lanceolate; bracts membraneous. Flowers in a loose inflorescence. Flowers with five perianth segments, the three sepals petal-like and longer than the petals; lip thick and velvety, entire or three-lobed, often with apical appendage more or less hairy and conspicuously marked to resemble the abdominal colours of various insects; no spur. Column with a terminal projection resembling a duck's head in profile; two stalked pollinia.

The genus *Ophrys* contains approximately thirty species distributed over Europe, western Asia and North Africa, with a centre of abundance in Mediterranean countries and islands. Some species exhibit extreme individual and geographical variation: this, plus hybridization between species, sometimes produces individual plants which are extremely difficult to identify.

**Cyprus Bee Orchid** *Ophrys kotschyi* Fleischm. et Soó
15-35cm. Leaves normally three to six, broadly lanceolate. Inflorescence lax, two to six flowered, not very variable; bracts equalling or longer than ovaries. Sepals green, the dorsal sepal normally curved forwards; petals half to two-thirds length of sepals, olive-green but sometimes brown or even red; lip blackish-maroon with white-edged elongated H-marking; side lobes distinctly reflexed. Differs from the closely related Cretan Bee Orchid in having all green sepals and the side lobes of the lip strongly reflexed. Species endemic to Cyprus, extremely local and uncommon, growing amongst low scrub on hillsides. Flowers March to April.

**Cretan Bee Orchid** *Ophrys cretica* (Vierh.) Nels.
20-30cm. Leaves three to six, broadly lanceolate. Inflorescence lax, two to eight flowered, not very variable; bracts longer than ovary. Sepals green or pinkish-green, the laterals dull pinkish on lower half; petals about half as long as sepals, reddish-green; lip blackish-maroon with white-bordered H-mark; side lobes not reflexed. Two not very well defined races have been described, differing mainly in lip markings, ssp. *naxia* Nels. from Naxos and ssp. *karpathensis* Nels. from Karpathos. *Ophrys cretica* differs from the Cyprus Bee Orchid in having a straight, up-pointing dorsal sepal, in its at least partially reddish-olive sepals and in its spreading side lobes. The nominate race is confined to Crete. Grows on hillsides amongst scrub and flowers from mid-March to April.

**Kurdish Bee Orchid** *Ophrys kurdica* Rückbr.
15-30cm. Leaves three to five, broadly lanceolate; inflorescence lax, three to seven flowered; bracts much longer than ovary. Sepals remarkably large and broad, greenish-pink to pink, the laterals down-pointing; petals about half length of sepals, green, brown or reddish, hairy; lip three-lobed, slender and curved inwards, side lobes small and recurved; lip markings whitish.
A recently described species known only from south-eastern Anatolia, Turkey, where it grows in damp grassland and hillside seepages. Flowers May.

Kurdish Bee Orchid

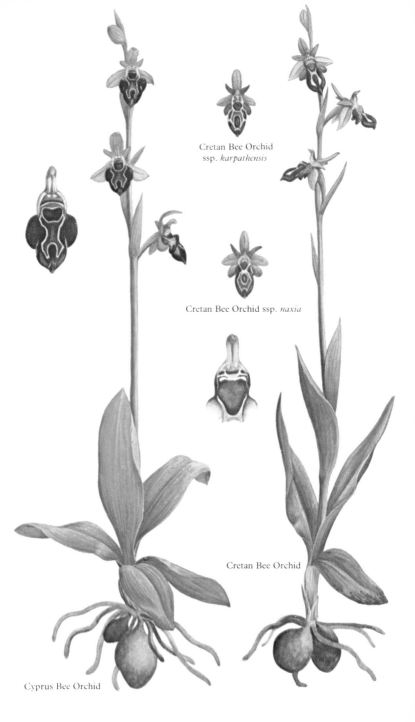

Cretan Bee Orchid
ssp. *karpathensis*

Cretan Bee Orchid ssp. *naxia*

Cretan Bee Orchid

Cyprus Bee Orchid

**Reinhold's Bee Orchid** *Ophrys reinholdii* Spruner ex Fleischm.
20-40cm. Leaves four to five, broadly lanceolate; bracts longer than ovary. Inflorescence lax, two to eight flowered. Sepals variable in colour, white, green, pink or even red; petals about half length of sepals, olive-brown to deep pink, recurved; lip three-lobed, dark maroon brown with restricted pale markings, sometimes reduced to two pale spots; side lobes strongly recurved. The ssp. *straussii* (Fleischm. et Bornm.) Nels. is not very well marked but usually has larger flowers, the lip side lobes are less recurved and the pale markings on the lip are larger.
Rhodes, Greece and south-western Turkey. The ssp. *straussii* has a more easterly distribution from southern Turkey to Syria, Iraq and Iran. Grows amongst scrub on hillsides and in coniferous woodland. Flowers late March to mid-May.

**Eyed Bee Orchid** *Ophrys argolica* Fleischm.
15-35cm. Leaves four to six, broadly lanceolate. Inflorescence lax, two to eight flowered, not varying greatly. Sepals deep pink, the dorsal sepal upright, sometimes recurved; petals about half as long as sepals and broad at base, rosy pink; lip normally entire, broad and rounded, red-brown to deep maroon with small eye pattern markings. The ssp. *elegans* (Renz) Nels. has a three-lobed lip with the side lobes recurved. In var. *flavescens* the sepals are white and the lip yellowish.
Central Greece, Crete, southern Turkey and Syria. Ssp. *elegans* is found in Cyprus. Grows in coniferous woodlands, on scrub-covered hillsides and rough grassland on calcareous soil. Flowers March and April.

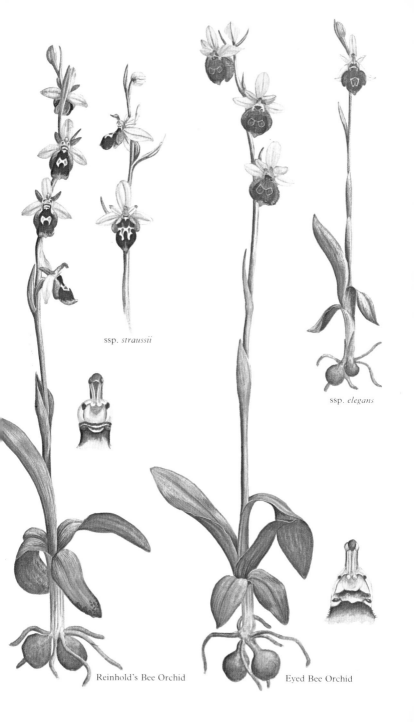

ssp. *straussii*

ssp. *elegans*

Reinhold's Bee Orchid

Eyed Bee Orchid

**Crescent Ophrys** *Ophrys lunulata* Parl.
30–40cm. Leaves up to seven or eight, lanceolate; bracts longer than ovary. Inflorescence lax, three to eight flowered, not variable. Sepals broad, pink with a green vein; petals long and slender, over two-thirds length of sepals, pink; lip three-lobed, long and slender with the sides strongly recurved, deep maroon-red with sickle-shaped blue marking near base and tip yellowish. Two forms have been described, var. *flavescens* Schulze with a yellow or greenish lip and a white crescent and var. *planimaculata* in which the lip may be bluish, brown or olive with a much more extensive pale area.
The Crescent Ophrys is found only in Sicily and Sardinia, growing amongst scrub or mixed scrub and grass on stony slopes; favours calcareous soils. Flowers March and April.

**Luristan Ophrys** *Ophrys luristanica* Renz.
25–65cm. Leaves four to seven, broadly lanceolate; bracts as long as ovary. Inflorescence lax, four to twelve flowered, not variable. Sepals large, recurved, pink to pinkish-violet; petals minute, only 1 to 1½mm long, pink; lip three-lobed, the side lobes very large, hollowed and directed upwards; lip deep maroon with large white markings. The combination of minute petals and very large side lobes prevents confusion with any other species.
A rare orchid known from southern Turkey and western Iran, in mountainous areas over 800 metres: also reputed to occur in northern Syria and in Iraq. In mountain grassland and scrub and oak scrub on limestone; flowers May and June.

**Mt Carmel Ophrys** *Ophrys carmelii* Fleischm. et Bornm.
[Syn. *O. scolopax* Cav. ssp. *attica* (Boiss. & Orph.) Nels.]
[Syn. *O. attica* (Boiss. et Orph.) Soó]
[Syn. *O. dinsmorei* Schltr.]
10–40cm. Leaves four to six, lanceolate; bracts longer than ovary. Inflorescence lax to rather dense, three to eight flowered. Sepals and petals ovate, green, rarely whitish; median sepal usually incurved; petals about half length of sepals; lip three-lobed, widest towards apex, variable in colour and pattern but similar to that of *O. scolopax* from which it may be distinguished by its green sepals and petals.
Occurs in southern Greece, Rhodes, Cyprus, western Turkey, Lebanon, Syria and Israel. In calcareous soils in sparse grassland, olive groves, maquis and forestry plantations; flowers early March to mid-April.

**Woodcock Orchid** *Ophrys scolopax* Cav.
French *Ophrys bécasse* or *Ophrys oiseau* Spanish *Flor de la abeja*
8–45cm. Leaves five to six, lanceolate to broadly lanceolate; bracts longer than ovary. An extremely variable species with several distinct races of widely differing character—incipient species might be a more accurate taxonomic term for some of these. However all races have a general resemblance in the lip, which is rotund with a forward pointing apical protuberance: brown or reddish-brown with a characteristic pattern of circles and lines, often enclosing a greyish-blue spot. In the nominate race the sepals are pink to pinkish-red and the petals also are pink to red.
Southern Spain, southern France, Italy, Corsica and Sardinia to central Greece and Cyprus. Grows in calcareous soils on scrub-covered hillsides, woodlands and sparsely grassed areas; flowers March and April.

Luristan Ophrys

Woodcock Orchid var.

Mt Carmel Ophrys var.

Mt Carmel Ophrys var.

Crescent Ophrys

Woodcock Orchid

Mt Carmel Ophrys

*Ophrys scolopax* Cav. ssp. *orientalis* (Renz) Nels. is close to nominate *scolopax* but has greenish-yellow or pinkish-white sepals and petals and the median sepal is curved forwards almost concealing the column; sepals broad, petals triangular; lip three-lobed, brown edged with yellow; apical appendage well developed, curved forwards and upwards.
Cyprus, southern and western Turkey, Lebanon and Israel. Flowers March to early April.

*Ophrys scolopax* Cav. ssp. *heldreichii* (Schltr.) Nels. is similar to nominate *scolopax* but flowers are much larger; sepals and petals normally pink.
South-western Turkey, Rhodes, Karpathos, Kos and Crete. Flowers late March and April.

*Ophrys scolopax* Cav. ssp. *cornuta* (Stev.) Camus has pink sepals and petals and is remarkable for the development of the side lobes of the lip. These are prolonged into forward pointing spurs 1cm long.
Locally in central, east and south-eastern Europe and northern Turkey. Flowers April and May.

*Ophrys scolopax* Cav. ssp. *oestrifera* (Bieb.) Soó from the Crimea and Caucasus is similar to *cornuta* but the lateral lobes of the lip have relatively small protuberances and the median lobe is oblong, wider than long.

*Ophrys scolopax* Cav. ssp. *apiformis* (Desf.) Maire et Weiller is the only member of the *scolopax* complex found in North Africa where it occurs in Morocco, Algeria and Tunisia. 15-40cm. Inflorescence lax, three to twelve flowered; sepals and petals red or white, rarely greenish; petals usually triangular, about half the length of sepals; lip three-lobed, the side lobes prolonged but not to the extent found in *cornuta*; median lobe greatly recurved; appendage large, pointing upwards and forwards. Flowers early March to April.

ssp. *apiformis*

ssp. *heldreichii*
var.

ssp. *heldreichii*
var.

ssp. *orientalis*

ssp. *orientalis*

ssp. *heldreichii*

ssp. *cornuta*

**Late Spider Orchid** *Ophrys fuciflora* (Crantz.) Moench.
French *Ophrys frelon* or *Ophrys bourdon* German *Hummelblume* Italian *Vesparia crestata*
15-55cm. Leaves four to seven, broadly lanceolate; bracts longer than ovary. Inflorescence lax, two to ten flowered. Flowers very variable and several distinct races recognized. The typical race has stout broad leaves and normally five to eight flowers. Sepals broad and usually rounded, pink or sometimes whitish with a green median line; petals about one-third length of sepals, flanged, pink; lip squarish three-lobed with large forward-pointing appendage; side lobes distinctly humped; colour dark brown to yellowish-brown with variable pale pattern.
Occurs in southern England (rare), eastern Spain, France, Germany, Italy and Albania; also central Czechoslovakia. Habitat, dry grassy areas, scrub and maquis thickets. Flowers March to May, earlier in the south, later in the north.

*Ophrys fuciflora* (Crantz.) Moench. ssp. *candica* Nels. [Syn. *O. arachnites* (Scop.) Lam.] has very short petals, about one-fifth the length of the sepals, and a broad lip with a distinctive rectangular whitish or yellowish pattern.
Recorded from Crete, Rhodes and the southern alpine region of Italy. Flowers mid-March to early May in Crete, late April to May in Italy.

*Ophrys fuciflora* (Crantz.) Moench. ssp. *oxyrrhynchos* (Tod.) Soó is remarkable for its green sepals and tiny green petals. The lip is variable in structure and there are two main colour forms, maroon-brown and yellowish-green.
Known only from Sicily and Sardinia where it flowers April to May.

Late Spider
Orchid

ssp. *candica*

ssp. *oxyrrhynchos*

ssp. *oxyrrhynchos*

*Ophrys fuciflora* (Crantz.) Moench. ssp. *exaltata* (Ten.) Nels. is a very distinct race, regarded by many botanists as a separate species. It is a large robust plant growing to 45cm with broadly lanceolate leaves. Inflorescence lax, three to eight flowered; bracts longer than ovary. Sepals normally pink with green veining but sometimes pinkish-green or deep mauve-pink; petals about half length of sepals, deep pink, sometimes pinkish-olive or pinkish-brown. Lip distinctive, three-lobed, long and relatively narrow with small side lobes; brown to maroon-brown with greatly reduced markings.

Corsica, Capri and central and southern Italy. Flowers from late March to April.

*Ophrys fuciflora* (Crantz.) Moench. ssp. *sundermannii* Soó [Syn. *O. fuciflora* (Crantz.) Moench. ssp. *pollinensis* Nels.] from Mt Gargano and Mt Pollino in east central Italy, has the sepals pink or white and the petals red; lip dark purplish-brown with a very small appendage. Rarely the sepals and petals are green. This orchid is very closely related to *exaltata*. Flowers late March to early June, depending upon altitude.

ssp. *exaltata* var.

ssp. *sundermannii* var.

ssp. *exaltata* var.

ssp. *sundermannii* var.

ssp. *exaltata*

ssp. *sundermannii*

**Short-Petalled Ophrys** *Ophrys fuciflora* (Crantz.) Moench. ssp. *bornmuelleri* (Schulze) B. et E. Willing [Syn. *O. bornmuelleri* Schulze]
10-30cm. Leaves four to six, broadly lanceolate; bracts slightly longer than ovary; inflorescence lax, two to five flowered, not very variable. Sepals broad, white to pale pink with green veining; petals extremely short, 1-2mm, pink; lip rich brown with restricted white-edged rectangular markings.
This orchid has an eastern Mediterranean range, in Cyprus, south-western Turkey, Lebanon and Israel. It is also reputed to occur on Rhodes. Habitat, grassy and scrub-covered hillsides, sometimes in forestry plantations and in olive groves on calcareous soil. Flowers mid-March to mid-April.

**Sawfly Orchid** *Ophrys tenthredinifera* Willd.
French *Ophrys guêpe* or *Ophrys porte-scie* Italian *Vesparia barbata*
10-40cm. Leaves six to nine, broadly lanceolate; bracts longer than ovary. Inflorescence lax, three to eight flowered. Flowers large and striking, not very variable. Sepals large and broad, pale to rich carmine-red with or without green veining; petals one-third length of sepals, broad and rounded, bright or dusky pink; lip large, rectangular, with side lobes reduced to rounded humps; central lobe flared towards apex, deeply notched by forward-pointing appendage; yellow or greenish-yellow, rarely pinkish-brown, with a small white-margined marking at the base. Widespread but local along the Mediterranean littoral from central and southern Portugal, Spain and eastwards to Turkey; also in North Africa. Habitat, grassy stony areas, scrub and maquis. Flowers March to May.

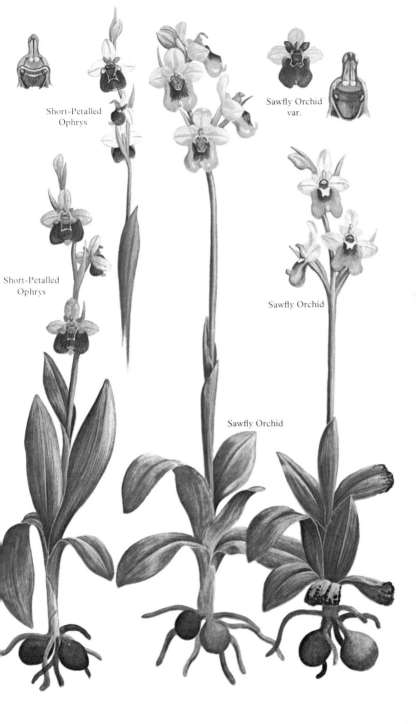

Short-Petalled
Ophrys

Sawfly Orchid
var.

Short-Petalled
Ophrys

Sawfly Orchid

Sawfly Orchid

**Bee Orchid** *Ophrys apifera* Huds.

15-50cm. Leaves five to nine, broadly lanceolate; bracts longer than the ovary. Inflorescence lax, two to ten flowered, not very variable. Sepals broad, normally pale or bright pink, sometimes whitish; petals variable, normally less than half the length of sepals, green or more rarely pink; lip oval with pronounced hairy side lobes; central lobe with greenish, backwards pointing appendage; deep red-brown with a variable yellow pattern. Several varieties have been described: f. *trollii* (Hegetschw.)? has a pointed lip and lacks the normal U-shaped lip marking, var. *bicolor* has a bicoloured green and red-brown lip without markings and var. *chlorantha* has whitish sepals and an all green lip.

Widely distributed in Europe except the north, from the British Isles eastwards and throughout the Mediterranean region including North Africa. Grows in a variety of habitats, grassland, woodland margins, scrub, sand-dune slacks and maquis. Flowers from May in the south to July in north of its range.

*Ophrys apifera* ssp. *jurana* Rupp. ex Zimm. [Syn. *O. apifera* var. *botteronii* (Chodat) A. & G.] has very large petals. *O. apifera* var. *friburgensis* Freyh. is similar, usually with slightly shorter petals, but is doubtfully distinct.

Found locally in west-central Europe and less frequently in southern Europe.

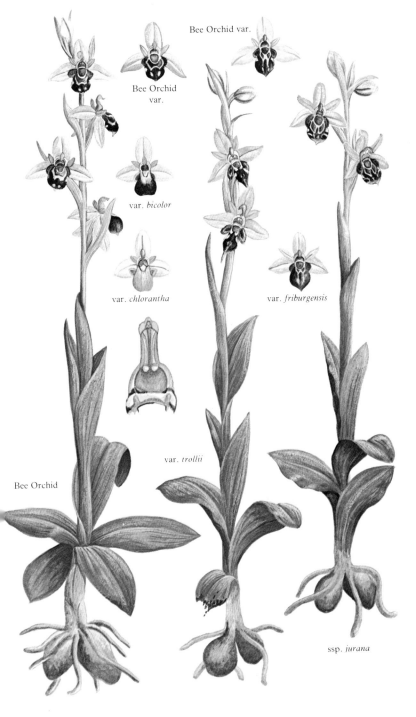

Bee Orchid var.

Bee Orchid var.

var. *bicolor*

var. *chlorantha*

var. *friburgensis*

var. *trollii*

Bee Orchid

ssp. *jurana*

**Bumble Bee Orchid** *Ophrys bombyliflora* Link.
French *Ophrys bourdon* or *Ophrys bombyx*
7-25cm. Tubers produced at the end of a root, one to several inches long. Leaves four to six, basal group horizontal, broadly lanceolate; bracts shorter than ovary. Inflorescence lax, one to five flowered, not very variable. Sepals broad, green; petals about one-third length of sepals, purplish-green; lip three-lobed, dark purplish-brown with restricted pale markings; side lobes in the form of large hairy lumps.
A local and uncommon species in the Mediterranean region from Portugal and Spain eastwards to southern Turkey, Lebanon and Israel; North Africa and the Canary Islands. Grows mainly in short grassland and in maquis. Flowers mid-March to late April.

**Horseshoe Orchid** *Ophrys ferrum-equinum* Desf.
French *Ophrys fer-à-cheval*
15-30cm. Leaves five to six, lanceolate to broadly lanceolate; bracts longer than ovary. Inflorescence lax, two to five large, widely spaced flowers; moderately variable. Sepals normally pink, sometimes red or reddish-brown; petals at least half length of sepals, sometimes wavy-edged, pink, red or pinkish-brown; lip purplish-brown with bluish markings in form of an inverted horseshoe, or two short lines. In var. *florescens?* the lip is yellow and the horseshoe marking whitish.
Southern Greece, Crete, the Aegean Islands, Rhodes and western and southern Turkey. In grassland amongst maquis and in pine woods on calcareous soils. Flowers March to May.

*Ophrys ferrum-equinum* ssp. *gottfriediana* (Renz) Nels. differs from the nominate race in having a longer, three-lobed lip and greenish-white or pale pink sepals; lateral sepals sometimes pinkish-brown on lower halves.
Recorded from some of the Greek Islands, including Paros, Siros, Kithira and Karpathos. The nominate race has also been recorded from the last named island. Flowers April.

**Bertoloni's Bee Orchid** *Ophrys bertolonii* Mor.
French *Ophrys de Bertoloni* German *Bertoloni Ragwurz* Italian *Ophrys Bertoloni*
15-35cm. Leaves five to seven, lanceolate to broadly lanceolate; bracts longer than ovary. Inflorescence lax, four to seven flowered, not very variable. Sepals white, pink or red, rarely greenish; petals half length of sepals, pink; lip large, entire or slightly three-lobed, depressed in centre like a saddle; purplish-black with a blue patch towards apex, sometimes ring-shaped. This is an uncommon orchid recorded from Spain, the Balearic Islands, southern France, southern Italy, Corsica, Sicily and Yugoslavia. Habitat, forest margins and clearings, dry grassland and amongst thickets. Flowers late March to end April.

Horseshoe Orchid
ssp. *gottfriediana*

Bertoloni's
Bee Orchid

Bumble Bee Orchid          Horseshoe Orchid

**Early Spider Orchid** *Ophrys sphegodes* Miller
French *Ophrys araignée* or *Oiseau-coquet* German *Spinnenblume* Italian *Calabrone*
10-45cm. Leaves five to nine, broadly lanceolate; bracts longer than ovary. Inflorescence lax, three to ten flowered, extremely variable with numerous described races. Nominate race, sepals large, green; petals about half length of sepals, green or slightly tinged reddish; lip ovoid, side lobes reduced to two humps, rich maroon-brown with a bluish H- or X-shaped marking. Widespread over western, central and southern Europe from southern England (rare), France, Italy, Corsica and the Balkans to northern Greece and the Crimea. Habitat, grasslands, maquis and woodland clearings on calcareous soils. Flowers early April to June, earlier in the south.

*Ophrys sphegodes* ssp. *mammosa* (Desf.) Soó has long sepals, green or sometimes laterals reddish on lower halves, rarely all pink; petals up to two-thirds length of sepals, often wavy edged, green or reddish; lip round to oblong, side lobes usually developed as forward projecting bosses. An eastern race recorded from Greece, western Turkey, Crete, Cyprus and Israel. Flowers end of February to April.

*Ophrys sphegodes* ssp. *atrata* (Lindl.) E. Mayer has large rounded or pointed sepals, green; petals broad with wavy edges, reddish-green and often edged red; lip side lobes well developed. Mediterranean region from Portugal and Spain eastwards to Yugoslavia. Flowers late March in south to May in north of range.

*Ophrys sphegodes tommasinii* (Vis) Soó from the coast of western Yugoslavia and north-western Greece is a three to five flowered form and has a rounded lip with an H-shaped patch.

*Ophrys sphegodes parnassica* (Vierh.) Soó has the lip dark brown margined with yellow; from Greece and Crete.

ssp. *mammosa* var.

ssp. *mammosa*

Early Spider Orchid

ssp. *mammosa*

ssp. *atrata*

*Ophrys sphegodes* ssp. *sintenisii* (Fleischm. et Bornm.) Nels. Similar to *O. s.* ssp. *mammosa* but with a more attenuated column shaped like a duck's head with a long bill; sepals bicoloured green and pinkish-green, usually longer and more pointed than in ssp. *mammosa*; lip three-lobed but side lobes not very large.
Cyprus, Turkey, Lebanon, Syria and Israel. Flowers mid-March to April.

*Ophrys sphegodes* ssp. *amanensis* Nels. is similar to *O.s.* ssp. *sintenisii* but sepals and petals uniform deep pink; the column is more attenuated; lip three-lobed, the side lobes well developed.
Found in southern Turkey; flowers May.

*Ophrys sphegodes* ssp. *garganica* Nels. is a large flowered form with green sepals and very broad green or brownish-green petals; lip rounded, entire, dark purplish-brown; lip markings two heavy parallel lines which meet at base. Sometimes considered merely a variant of nominate *sphegodes*.
Spain and central and southern Italy; flowers March and early April.

*Ophrys sphegodes* ssp. *provincialis* Nels. has the sepals green or pinkish, petals green or brownish-green. Not unlike a smaller edition of *O.s* ssp. *garganica*, it too is sometimes viewed as no more than a variant of nominate *sphegodes*.
Distribution, restricted to southern France; flowers March.

*Ophrys sphegodes* ssp. *aesculapii* (Renz.) Soó may be recognized by its very broad yellow lip margin. Sepals and petals green to brownish-green; lip marking in the form of an elongated H.
Known only from Greece (Attika and Peloponnese). Flowers March and April.

*Ophrys sphegodes* ssp. *sipontensis* Gump. has the sepals white or pink, laterals red on lower halves; lip entire, very dark brown with hairy edge; marking H-shaped, blue with pale edging.
Known only from Mt Gargano in southern Italy; flowers in April and May.

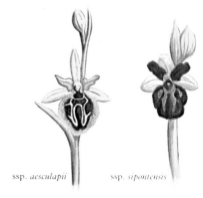

ssp. *aesculapii*        ssp. *sipontensis*

ssp. *amanensis*

ssp. *sintenisii*

ssp. *provincialis*

ssp. *garganica*

*Ophrys sphegodes* ssp. *litigiosa* (Camus) Becherer is a small flowered race; sepals green, normal rounded, the laterals drooping; petals broad, green; lip purplish-brown edged with greenish yellow; side lobes not strongly developed; blue lip markings small.
Known from Spain, France, Corfu, Crete and Greece. Flowers March to mid-April.

*Ophrys sphegodes* ssp. *sicula* Nels. is a robust race, the inflorescence carrying from five to fifteen flowers. Sepals and petals whitish-pink to deep pink; petals two-thirds length of sepals; lip slightly three-lobed, much recurved; markings restricted to two short lines which are connected at base. This rather poorly defined race occurs alongside other forms of *sphegodes* and hybridization is frequent.
Known only from Sicily and southern Italy; flowers March.

**Grecian Spider Orchid** *Ophrys spruneri* Nyman.
Differs from *O. sphegodes* in being two to four flowered and in having normally rounded sepals with laterals drooping, deep pink with a median green vein, green or purplish-green; petals long, pink; lip dark purplish-brown, ovoid, three-lobed, the side lobes in the form of long drooping arms.
Known from southern Greece, the Aegean and Crete. Grows in grassy areas and in maquis; flowers March and April.

*Ophrys spruneri* ssp. *panormitana* (Tod.) Soó has variable sepals and petals, from whitish to deep carmine-red; lip three-lobed, dark red-brown rarely edged yellow; lip marking X-shaped with central circle.
Known from Sicily; flowers March.

Early Spider
Orchid
ssp. *sicula*

Grecian Spider
Orchid
ssp. *panormitana*

Grecian Spider Orchid

Early Spider Orchid
ssp. *litigiosa*

**False Spider Orchid** *Ophrys arachnitiformis* Gren. & Phil.
French *Ophrys en forme d'araignée* German *Spinnenformige Ragwurz*
15-40cm. A thickset species which may perhaps be of hybrid origin, with three to seven large broadly lanceolate leaves; bracts large, twice length of ovary. Inflorescence lax, three to six flowered and very variable. Sepals large, more or less rounded, pink or deep carmine-pink with a green median vein; petals half to two-thirds length of sepals, pink to carmine-pink; lip variable, oblong to squarish with reduced side lobes, rich reddish-brown with variable H- or X-shaped pattern.
An uncommon Mediterranean species found from Spain to France (Nice, Toulon, Var), Italy and Yugoslavia; also Sicily, Sardinia and Algeria. Grows in undisturbed pasture and grassy areas and in maquis. Flowers mid-March to end April.

**Sombre Bee Orchid** *Ophrys fusca* Link
French *Ophrys sombre* Germany *Ragwurz* Italian *Moscaria giallognola*
10-40cm. Leaves four to six, lanceolate to broadly lanceolate; bracts longer than ovary. Inflorescence lax, two to eight flowered. This species is split into three markedly different races which have the appearance of distinct species. In the nominate race the sepals are green to yellowish-green, the dorsal sepal curved forwards; petals about two-thirds length of sepals, green sometimes tinged yellow or brown; lip three-lobed, the side lobes variable, well developed or undeveloped, central lobe indented; lip brown with narrow yellowish margin, two blue patches near base.
This is one of the commonest Mediterranean *Ophrys*, found throughout the region and in Portugal and south-western Rumania. Grows on limestone hillsides amongst maquis and in olive orchards. Flowers February to April.

*Ophrys fusca* ssp. *iricolor* (Desf.) O. Schwarz is most distinct having much larger flowers; lip 2cm long with a bright blue patch; side lobes well developed but shorter than in the closely related *O. fusca* ssp. *atlantica;* petals reddish-green.
This race occurs in Italy (Riviera and Mt Argentario), Yugoslavia and Greece to Turkey, Lebanon and Israel; also Cyprus, Crete, Rhodes, the Greek Islands and North Africa. Flowers April.

*Ophrys fusca* ssp. *omegaifera* (Fleischm.) Nels. has the lip arched and barely indented at apex with a yellowish W-marking instead of a blue patch; flowers normally one to three.
Southern Spain, Balearic Islands, Morocco, Crete, Rhodes, Turkey and Lebanon. Flowers early, from late December to March.

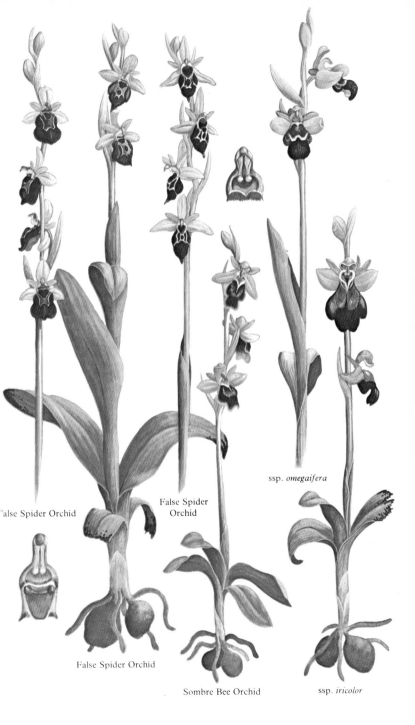

False Spider Orchid

False Spider Orchid

False Spider Orchid

ssp. *omegaifera*

False Spider Orchid

Sombre Bee Orchid

ssp. *iricolor*

**Moroccan Ophrys** *Ophrys fusca* ssp. *atlantica* (Munby) E. E. et A. Camus
15-25cm. Leaves four to seven, broadly lanceolate; bracts longer than ovary. Inflorescence lax, two to three flowered, not very variable. Sepals long, green; petals about three-quarters length of sepals, green; lip three-lobed, the side lobes nearly as long as the central lobe; purplish-black with blue patch at base. Long side lobes distinguish this subspecies from *Ophrys fusca* ssp. *iricolor*.
High mountains of Morocco and southern Spain. Flowers later than *Ophrys fusca* ssp. *iricolor*, late April to June.

**Yellow Bee Orchid** *Ophrys lutea* (Gouan) Cav.
French *Ophrys jaune* German *Gelbe Ragwurz* Italian *Ophrys giallo*
10-30cm. Leaves four to eight, broadly lanceolate; bracts longer than ovary. Inflorescence lax, two to seven flowered, moderately variable. Sepals green, the central one curved forwards; petals about half the length of sepals, yellowish-green; lip three-lobed, side lobes well developed and median lobe indented at apex; broad yellow margin surrounding central reddish-brown area and blue or sometimes yellow basal patches. Two well-marked subspecies are recognized. A common species found in suitable area throughout the Mediterranean region, including North Africa, Cyprus, Turkey and Lebanon. The nominate race is dominant in southern France, Sicily, Sardinia and the Aegean Islands. Flowers during March and April, grows in maquis and grassy areas.

*Ophrys lutea* ssp. *murbeckii* (Fleischm.) Soó [Syn. *O. lutea* var. *minor* Guss] occurs throughout the range of the species. It has a smaller lip than typical *lutea* (9-12mm against 12-18mm) and a much smaller central lobe with an inverted V at base.

*Ophrys lutea* ssp. *melena* Renz from Greece has the broad edges of the lip brown with blackish-purple hairs and the rest of the lip dark purplish-brown except the blue basal patch. Similar in general appearance to *Ophrys fusca* from which it may be distinguished by the lip shape, which is flat or curved slightly upwards whilst in *O. fusca* the lip is curved downwards.

var.

var.

var.

ssp. *murbeckii*

Moroccan Ophrys

Yellow Bee Orchid

ssp. *melena*

**Pale Ophrys** *Ophrys pallida* Rafin.
10-20cm. Leaves four to seven, short, broadly lanceolate; bracts longer than ovary. Inflorescence lax, two to five flowered, not very variable. Sepals broad, pinkish-white or sometimes greenish-white; petals about half length of sepals, green; lip rectangular, shallowly three-lobed, much incurved with apex pointing inwards; maroon-brown with pinkish-white to blue-grey patches at base.
An uncommon species known from Tunisia and Algeria in North Africa, Sicily and probably Sardinia. Grows on grassy slopes and in maquis; flowers March and April.

**Mirror Orchid, Mirror of Venus** *Ophrys speculum* Link
French *Ophrys miroir*
10-30cm. Leaves five to seven, broadly lanceolate; bracts longer than ovary. Inflorescence lax, three to eight flowered, not very variable. Sepals green with red-brown stripes, the dorsal sepal curved forwards; petals small, about one-third length of sepals or shorter, brown, recurved; lip three-lobed, edges densely hairy, rich purplish-brown with a large shining blue centre. In *O. speculum* var. *regis-ferdinandii* (Acht et Kell.) Soó, from Rhodes and western Turkey, the side lobes are very reduced and the edges of the lip strongly recurved so that the lip appears almost completely blue.
A Mediterranean species, locally common; recorded from Spain and Italy, eastwards to Greece, Turkey, Lebanon and Israel; Balearic Islands, Corsica, Sardinia, Sicily and Rhodes; also North Africa in Morocco, Algeria and Tunisia. Grows in undisturbed grassy areas, light woodland and maquis. Flowers March and April.

*Ophrys speculum* ssp. *lusitanica* Danesch from Portugal has long side lobes and marginal hairs on the lip dark yellow or rusty-brown. This is a more robust plant than the nominate race, growing to 50cm and the inflorescence up to fifteen flowered.

**Fly Orchid** *Ophrys insectifera* L.
French *Ophrys mouche* German *Fliegenblume* Italian *Pecchie*
20-50cm. Leaves seven to nine, broadly lanceolate, growing up stem, not forming a rosette at base as in most *Ophrys* species; bracts longer than ovary. Inflorescence lax, two to sixteen flowered, not variable. Sepals green; petals very slender, half length of sepals, dark red-brown; lip three-lobed, the central lobe elongated and indented, velvety dark brown with a rectangular greyish-blue patch at base. *O. insectifera* var. *ochroleuca* (Camus)? has lip yellow or greenish and a whitish basal patch.
Ranges further north than any other species of *Ophrys*, from central and southern Scandinavia and the British Isles throughout much of Europe north of the Mediterranean, eastwards to Russia; absent from south-eastern Europe and rare in north and extreme south of its range. Occurs up to 1500 metres in mountains. Grows in undisturbed pastures, pine and beech woodland and at the edge of thickets on limestone soils. Flowers May to July depending on latitude and altitude.

Mirror Orchid
ssp. *lusitanica*

Pale Ophrys

Mirror Orchid
var.
*regis-ferdinandii*

Fly Orchid

Fly Orchid
albino form

Mirror Orchid

# Tongue Orchids *Serapias*

Perennials, 15-30(60)cm. Tubers two to five, rounded to ovoid, undivided. Leaves narrow, channelled and pointed, often curved inwards or outwards; perianth with three outer segments (sepals) partially fused, forming with the petals a pointed helmet; lip long, triangular and tongue-like with two basal lobes which curve upwards, partly concealed within the helmet; no spur. Column with a long beak.

The genus *Serapias* comprises some seven species and is most abundant in the Mediterranean region. Hybridization between species is not uncommon, and hybrids between *Serapias*, *Orchis* and other genera have been recorded.

### Long-Lipped Serapias *Serapias vomeracea* (Burm.) Briq.
French *Serapias à long labelle* German *Bartige Stendelwurz*
20-60cm. Leaves six to eight, long, narrow, channelled and pointed, reflexed outwards; basal sheaths green, unspotted; bracts longer than the flower. Inflorescence four to ten flowered, fairly widely spaced; lip longer than the helmet, narrowing at base and with two more or less parallel humps in the throat; hood pale red with darker veining, lip deep reddish-brown. This species may be distinguished from *S. lingua* and *S. parviflora* (which also have the lip narrowing at base) in having the bracts longer than the flowers.
Widespread throughout most of the Mediterranean area, also in Turkey and Lebanon to the Caucasus. Habitat, moist areas including woodlands, grassland and seepages on hill slopes. Flowers late March to early June, depending on latitude and altitude.

### Eastern Serapias *Serapias orientalis* Nels. = *S. cordigera* L.
15-35cm. Leaves moderately long and broad, five to seven in number; bracts longer than helmet. Inflorescence relatively dense, five to seven flowered. Lip broad, only slightly more slender at base, yellowish to reddish-buff, with two parallel humps in throat. A dark-flowered form has been named var. *cordigeroides* Nels. Similar to *S. neglecta* but that species has the lip narrowed at base and occurs in a different region.
Southern Greece and the Greek Islands, Cyprus and southern Turkey, growing mainly on calcareous soils in wet meadows, olive groves and maquis. Flowers from late March to early May.

*Serapias orientalis* ssp. *apulica* Nels. = *S. cordigera* L. grows on Mt Gargano in south-eastern Italy. It is distinguished by its larger flowers. It flowers mid-March to April.

ssp. *apulica*

Long-lipped Serapias      Eastern Serapias      var. *cordigeroides*

**Scarce Serapias** *Serapias neglecta* De Not.
French *Serapias négligé*
10-30cm. Leaves four to ten, narrowly lanceolate to moderately broad, channelled, more or less recurved; basal sheaths green, unspotted; bracts not longer than helmet. Inflorescence rather dense, normally four to six flowered; lip large, an elongated oval, usually pale red-brown merging to yellowish in centre; rarely the flowers are red; two parallel humps in throat.
Southern France, northern Italy, Corsica, Sardinia and probably Sicily to south-western Yugoslavia. An uncommon and local species growing in damp meadows, light woodland and maquis, mainly on slightly acid soils. Flowers end of March to April.

*Serapias neglecta* ssp. *ionica* Nels. is a smaller, red-flowered race found on the Ionian Islands where it grows in damp pastures on sandy soil; flowers April.

ssp. *ionica*

Scarce Serapias

**Heart-Flowered Serapias** *Serapias cordigera* L.
French *Serapias en coeur* German *Herzformige Stendelwurz* Italian *Satirio-barbone*
15-45cm. Leaves five to eight, lanceolate, channelled, more or less speckled with deep red on
basal sheaths; bracts average shorter than helmet. Inflorescence rather dense, two to ten
flowered. Lip heart-shaped, hairy, deep purplish-maroon with fine blackish streaks. A smaller,
pale red form from North Africa has been described as var. *mauretanica* (E. G. Cam.) Nels.
Distribution, throughout the Mediterranean area from Spain to Greece, North Africa and the
Azores. Grows in grassland, sandy heaths, woodland and maquis, flowering late March to May.

**Small-Flowered Serapias** *Serapias parviflora* Parl.
French *Serapias à petites fleurs*
10-35cm. Leaves five to seven, linear-lanceolate, channelled and curved inwards, usually red-
speckled at base; bracts equalling or shorter than helmet. Inflorescence lax, four to twelve
flowered in an elongated spike; flowers small, lip pale red with darker veins, incurved. Eastern
Mediterranean plants are often separated as a distinct race, *S. parviflora* ssp. *laxiflora* (Chaub.)
Soó: this is usually a more robust plant with wider leaves and normally a greenish-yellow lip.
Found locally from Portugal, Spain and Italy to Greece, southern Turkey, North Africa and
the Canary Islands. Grows in both wet and dry grasslands, sand-dune slacks and olive groves.
Flowers late March to early May.

albino form

Heart-Flowered
Serapias

Heart-Flowered
Serapias
var. *mauretanica*

Small-Flowered
Serapias
ssp. *laxiflora*

Small-Flowered
Serapias

**Hybrid Serapias** *Serapias olbia* Verg.
10-25cm. Normally has three, not two tubers. Leaves narrowly lanceolate and whole plant
slender; bracts shorter than the helmet. Inflorescence lax, two to five flowered; lip very dark
purplish-red, hairy. A paler red-flowered form has been named var. *gregaria* (Godf.) Nels. It is
generally accepted that *S. olbia* is of hybrid origin, probably between *S. cordigera* and *S. lingua*.
A rare species known only from a restricted range at Var in south-eastern France. Grows in
acid soils in maritime sand slacks and lake edges, flowering mid-April to mid-May.

**Tongue Orchid** *Serapias lingua* L.
French *Serapias à langue* German *Zungen-Stendelwurz* Italian *Satirio incappuciato*
10-30cm. Tubers two, three or more at the end of short stolons. Leaves four to five, linear to
lanceolate, basal sheaths green, unspotted; bracts normally shorter than or equalling helmet.
Inflorescence elongated, lax, two to eight flowered. Lip variable in colour, yellowish, violet-pink
or even dark red; central lobe much elongated; a single hump at base with a longitudinal furrow.
A common species, often in colonies, in the Mediterranean area, south-western Europe and
North Africa, as far east as Greece. Grows in both dry and wet grasslands, olive groves, woodland
and maquis. Flowers March to early May.

# Man Orchid *Aceras*

Perennial. 10-40cm. Tubers two, ovoid, undivided. Keeled glossy leaves with a long spike of
15mm long flowers. Perianth segments curved inwards forming a helmet; lip with two slender
lateral lobes and central lobe divided into narrow apical lobes—the 'man's' arms and legs.
No spur. Column very short. The single species is widespread but local in western Europe
and the Mediterranean; rare in Britain. The Man Orchid may be distinguished from the
several species of *Orchis* with similar lip structures by its lack of a spur.

**Man Orchid** *Aceras anthropophorum* (L.) R. Br.
French *L' homme pendu* German *Menschentragendes Ohnhorn* Italian *Ballerino*
10-40cm. Leaves five to six, lanceolate, unspotted; bracts shorter than ovary. Inflorescence a
long narrow spike with numerous flowers. Sepals and petals incurved forming a hood; lip
three-lobed, the middle lobe deeply split and the lateral lobes long and slender. The usual
colour of the flowers is yellow or greenish-yellow, margined and streaked with red. The Man
Orchid may be distinguished from somewhat similar *Orchis* species by the lack of a spur.
Found over much of the southern half of Europe from southern England (rare) and the
Netherlands to Greece, Rhodes, Cyprus and North Africa. Grows in calcareous soils from
sea level up to 1500 metres, in pastures, woodland edges and in olive groves; flowers from late
March to June. Frequently hybridizes with various species of *Orchis*.

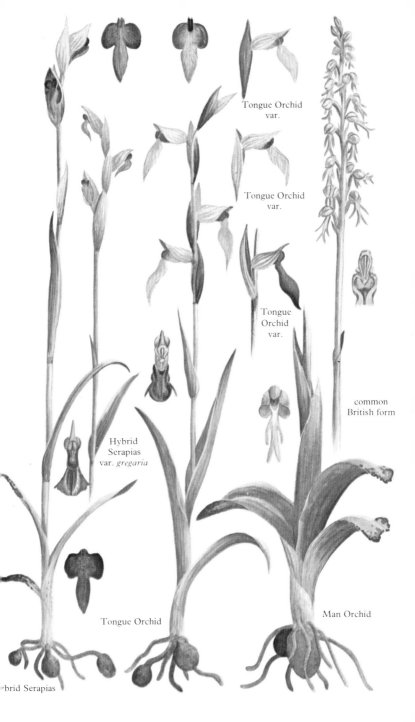

Tongue Orchid
var.

Tongue Orchid
var.

Tongue
Orchid
var.

common
British form

Hybrid
Serapias
var. *gregaria*

Tongue Orchid

Man Orchid

brid Serapias

## Lizard Orchids *Himantoglossum*

Sometimes included under the genus *Loroglossum*. Perennials. 30-90cm. Tubers two, elliptic. Striking robust orchids with oblong leaves narrowed at base and tips; flowering spike loosely many flowered. Perianth segments incurved, forming a hood; lip three-lobed, the central lobe often greatly elongated, twisting, and bifurcated at tip. Spur short; column stumpy. Some species with a strong goat-like smell. The nominate *Himantoglossum hircinum* is widespread in southern Europe, though sparse and local. The remaining species are extremely local and uncommon with restricted distributions.

**Lizard Orchid** *Himantoglossum hircinum* (L.) W. D. J. Koch
French *Orchis bouc* German *Riemenzunge*
One of the larger and more robust European orchids, 30-75cm. Leaves six to eight, oblong or broadly lanceolate, the lower ones often withered; bracts equalling or slightly longer than ovary. Inflorescence moderately dense and many flowered. Sepals and petals incurved, forming a hood, greenish or greyish-green with reddish streaking; lip three-lobed, the central lobe extremely elongated and strap-like, bifurcated at tip, coiled when in bud; lateral lobes shorter; lip variable in colour, whitish, greenish, olive-brown to rarely pale pink, with red spots at base; spur short and conical, pointing downwards, 1.5 to 2.5mm long. Flowers smell strongly of goat, especially towards dusk.
Local and uncommon over much of the southern half of Europe, from southern Britain and Netherlands to France, Germany, Spain, Italy, Czechoslovakia, Hungary and Yugoslavia; also Balearic Islands, Corsica, Sardinia, Sicily and North Africa. Grows in calcareous soils in light woodland, edges of thickets, sand-dunes and grassland, especially grassy banks with scattered shrubs. Flowers late May to July or even August.

var.

var.

var.

Lizard Orchid

*Himantoglossum hircinum* ssp. *caprinum* (Bieb.) Sunderm
Differs from the nominate race in having inflorescence less dense, the spur longer, 3-5mm, and the helmet more elongated. Lip normally bright pink with red speckling at base, deeply divided at apex of median lobe (*ca.* 15mm).
Found in the Crimea and northern Turkey. There are also records of plants attributed to this race from Yugoslavia, Greece, Crete and Bulgaria. Grows in calcareous soils in rough pastures, woodland margins and clearings and scrub-covered hillsides; flowers May to early July.

ssp. *caprinum*

**Beck's Lizard Orchid** *Himantoglossum hircinum* ssp. *calcaratum* (G. Beck) Soó
40-90cm. An even more robust plant than the common Lizard Orchid, of which it is considered
to be a subspecies. Leaves eight to ten, broadly lanceolate; bracts slightly longer than ovary.
Flowers large and showy with the central lobe of the lip 8-10cm long, bifurcated deeply at tip;
spur well developed, 8-12mm long. Flowers reddish-violet with darker spotting at base of lip.
Confined to mountainous areas in southern Yugoslavia where it grows at altitudes of 400-1000
metres, in mountain pastures and edges of thickets on calcareous soils. Flowers June to August,
depending upon altitude.

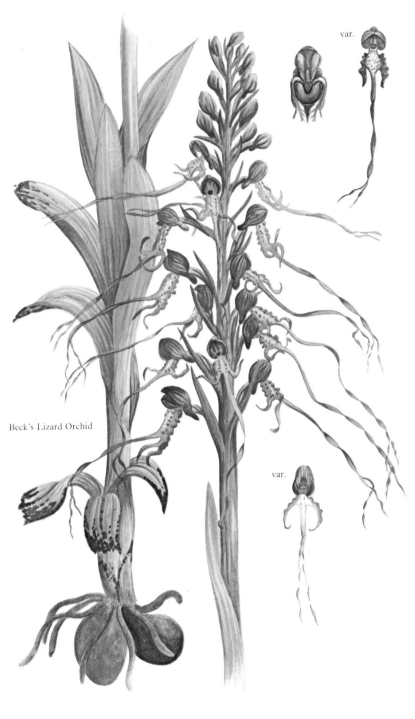

var.

Beck's Lizard Orchid

var.

**Short-Lobed Lizard Orchid** *Himantoglossum affine* (Boiss.) Schltr.
30-60cm. Leaves seven to nine, broadly lanceolate; bracts slightly longer than ovary. Inflorescence lax, ten to thirty flowered. Flowers mainly greenish-white and olive-brown, normally not marked with red; lip relatively short, 2-4cm, only moderately bifurcated at tip; side lobes very short, stumpy and sometimes even absent; lip not spotted at base; spur 3-6mm long.
A rare and very local species known from western and southern Turkey, Lebanon, Syria, Iraq and Iran. Grows on calcareous soils in pine forests, oak woods and hillside pasture amongst scrub. Flowers mid-May to July.

Short-Lobed Lizard Orchid

**Caucasian Lizard Orchid** *Himantoglossum formosum* (Stev.) C. Koch
50-70cm. Leaves six to eight, broadly lanceolate; bracts longer than ovary. Inflorescence
moderately lax, 15-30 flowered. Lip relatively short and central lobe notched; side lobes
much reduced; flowers greenish-white, sepals streaked brown to reddish-brown; lip mainly
white, edged olive-brown; spur slender, 9-10mm long.
A rare species of which little is known, recorded from mountain woodland and scrub on calcareous soils in the eastern Caucasus and south-eastern Transcaucasia. Flowers May and June.

Caucasian Lizard Orchid

## Giant Orchid *Barlia*

Perennial. 30-80cm. Tubers large, ovoid, undivided. A very massive orchid with large broad basal leaves and long bracts. Flower spike dense and cylindrical. Perianth, lateral sepals spreading, dorsal sepal and petals slightly incurved to form loose helmet; lip three-lobed, the lateral lobes broad and sickle-shaped, the central lobe divided into two thick arms; spur short, conical and down-pointing.

The single species is distributed locally through the Mediterranean area and in North Africa. This is one of the earliest orchids to flower, sometimes blooming in late December.

**Giant Orchid** *Barlia robertiana* (Loisel.) Greuter
[Syn. *Himantoglossum longibracteatum* (Biv.) Schltr.]
French *Orchis géant* or *Orchis à longues bractées* Italian *Giglio bratteoso*
30-80cm. An extremely robust orchid with succulent broadly lanceolate leaves; bracts twice as long as ovary. Inflorescence dense and many flowered. Lateral sepals more or less spreading, dorsal sepal and petals curved inwards to form a helmet; lip three-lobed, the side lobes curved and wavy at edges; central lobe deeply indented to form two thick arms; spur short and conical, down-pointing. Flowers greyish to greenish-white, tinged brown or red; lip variable in colour and markings. The flowers have an iris-like scent. Rarely the flowers may be entirely white and without markings—var. *candida* (Soó)?
A widespread Mediterranean species ranging from Portugal and Spain to Turkey and North Africa; also known from the Canary Islands. It grows on neutral soils in grassy places, woodland thickets and scrub-covered hillsides; one of the earliest orchids to flower, from late December to early April.

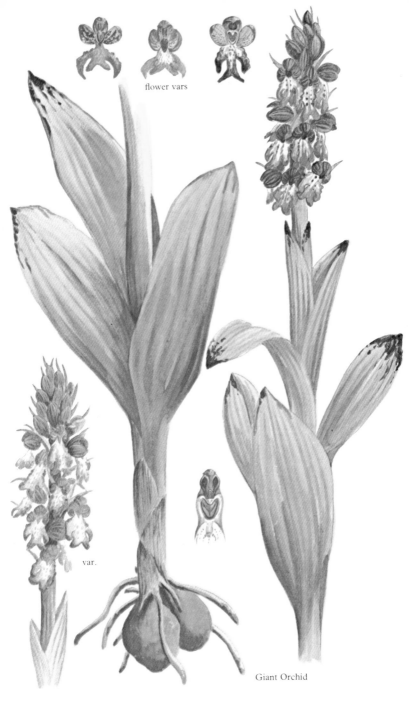

flower vars

var.

Giant Orchid

# Pyramidal Orchid *Anacamptis*

Perennial. 20-50cm. Tubers two, ovoid, undivided. Leaves narrow, keeled and acuminate at tips; flower-head conical, densely packed with 12mm flowers; bracts membranous, small and inconspicuous. Perianth, lateral sepals spreading, dorsal sepal and petals incurved forming a hood; lip three-lobed with two longitudinal ridges towards base; spur very long, slender and slightly curved.

The single species is widely distributed over most of Europe.

**Pyramidal Orchid** *Anacamptis pyramidalis* (L.) Rich
French *Orchis pyramidal* German *Spitzorchis* or *Hundswurz*

20-50cm. A slender plant with five to eight linear to lanceolate, unspotted leaves; bracts about same length as ovary. Inflorescence, a very dense conical flower-head, expanding to an oblong shape as flowers open. Flowers pale to dark pink. Lateral sepals widely spread, dorsal sepal and petals incurved forming a hood; lip three lobed, at the base of the lip there are two small erect ridges which help insects to locate the aperture of the spur: spur down-curved, long and very slender, normally longer than the ovary.

Three varieties have been named: var. *brachystachys* Boiss. from mountain pastures in the eastern Mediterranean is smaller with a rounder flower-head and pale pink blossoms; flowers from February to April. Var. *tanayensis* Chenev. from the Alps between 1200 and 2000 metres, described from Lake Tanay, has dark purple flowers and the spur shorter than the ovary. Flowers in May. Var *albiflora* (Raulin)? has white flowers.

Ranges throughout most of Europe south of southern Sweden and central Russia; also in North Africa, Asia Minor and Israel, eastwards to Iran and the Caucasus. Common in Britain north to southern Scotland and the Hebrides. Habitat, dry grassy slopes mainly on calcareous soils.

# Dense-Flowered Orchid *Neotinea*

Perennial. 10-30cm. Tubers two, ovoid, undivided. Two or three spotted or unspotted bluish-green leaves, large in relation to size of flowers. Flower spike dense with numerous 7mm flowers. Perianth segments incurved to form a hood; lateral sepals and petals fused at base; lip three lobed; spur very short, conical and down-pointing.

The single species has a limited mainly southern distribution.

**Dense-Flowered Orchid** *Neotinea maculata* (Desf.) Stearn
[Syn. *Neotinea intacta* (Link) Reichb.]
French *Orchis intact* Italian *Satirione macchiato*

10-30cm. Leaves five to seven, the lower broadly lanceolate, the upper more elongate, rather dark bluish-green to even reddish, spotted or immaculate; bracts very short. Inflorescence tightly packed, flowers small, pale dusky pink to yellowish or greenish-white. Sepals and petals forming a helmet; lip flat, three-lobed, the central lobe toothed at apex; spur very short, down-pointing. The flowers have a delicate vanilla scent.

From western Ireland (Co. Clare, Mayo and Galway), Canary Islands, Madeira and North Africa and throughout the Mediterranean littoral to Turkey and Lebanon. It grows in wooded country, maquis and on stony slopes on slightly acid and limestone soils. Flowers March to May.

Pyramidal Orchid
var. *brachystachys*

Dense-Flowered Orchid

Pyramidal Orchid

Dense-Flowered Orchid spotted leaved form

## Ground Orchids *Orchis*

Perennials. 10-50(80)cm. Tubers usually two, rounded or ovoid, undivided. Leaves variable spotted or unspotted. Perianth, sepals and petals all incurving forming a hood, or with the two lateral sepals spreading and the dorsal sepal and petals incurving, forming the helmet. Lip variable, may be entire but in most cases three or four lobed; spur present; bracts thin, membranous. The similar genus *Dactylorhiza* differs in having divided, palmate tubers and thicker leaf-like bracts.

One of the best-known groups of terrestrial orchids, upwards of twenty species found in Europe, many of them common and widespread.

### Bug Orchid *Orchis coriophora* L.

French *Orchis punaise* German *Wanzen-orchis* Italian *Cimiciattola*

15-45cm. Basal leaves five to six, lanceolate, channelled, higher leaves enclosing stem; bracts as long as ovary. Inflorescence a fairly dense cylindrical spike. Sepals and petals forming a helmet ending in a spike; lip three lobed, curved slightly inwards; central lobe only a little longer than side lobes; side lobes not toothed; spur slightly shorter than ovary, pointing downwards. Flowers dusky purplish-red with green streaks or white or greenish-white marked with red. The whole plant has an offensive odour similiar to squashed bed bugs.

Mainly central Europe from France eastwards to southern Germany, the lower slopes of the Alps, Poland, Czechoslovakia, Hungary, Yugoslavia and Russia. Grows in damp grasslands normally on slightly acid soils. This is a species which appears to be decreasing in Europe although the following race is still widespread and common. Flowers between late April and June.

*Orchis coriophora* ssp. *fragrans* (Poll.) Richter differs in having a longer central lobe to the lip, bracts whitish and the flowers paler, mainly pink and white, and pleasantly scented.

This race has a Mediterranean distribution, North Africa, Spain and eastwards to Greece, Cyprus, Turkey, Lebanon and the Crimea. Grows both in damp pasture and on grassy hillsides and amongst maquis. Flowers April to early June.

### Holy Orchid *Orchis sancta* L.

15-45cm. Similar in habit to *Orchis coriophora*: leaves five to seven, linear to lanceolate; bract longer than ovary. Inflorescence slightly more lax than the Bug Orchid and flowers larger pale pink to bright red; lip three-lobed, the side lobes strongly toothed; spur as long as ovary curved downwards.

Aegean Islands, Turkey, Syria, Lebanon and Israel, growing on calcareous soils in dry grass land, sandy areas and amongst maquis. Flowers April.

Bug Orchid
ssp. *fragrans*

Holy Orchid

Bug Orchid

**Burnt Orchid** *Orchis ustulata* L.
French *Orchis brûlé* German *Schwarzköpfige Orchis* Italian *Sipho macchiettato*
10-25cm. Leaves five to seven, broadly lanceolate, unspotted; bracts shorter than ovary. Inflorescence dense, flowers small; buds purplish-black with the appearance of being scorched. Sepals and petals much incurved forming a rounded helmet; lip three-lobed, side lobes spread outwards, central lobe deeply indented; spur down-curved, about half length of ovary. Hood deep purplish, lip white, sparsely spotted with red. Flowers slightly scented. Var. *albiflora* (Thielens)? has a white lip without red spots and the hood is paler.
Common and widespread over much of Europe, including the British Isles, except in the far north and extreme south, eastwards to Russia and the Caucasus. Grows on chalk downs and mountain and subalpine meadows up to 2000 metres. Flowers April to August depending on altitude and latitude.

**Toothed Orchid** *Orchis tridentata* Scop.
French *Orchis dentelé* German *Dreizähniges Orchis*
15-40cm. Leaves six to eight, oblong-lanceolate, unspotted; bracts less than half length of ovary. Inflorescence moderately dense. Sepals and petals forming a hood, the sepals tapering into long points; lip three-lobed, lateral lobes spreading, central lobe bifurcated with a small tooth in centre; spur as long as ovary, curved downwards. Flowers variable, pale red, violet, lilac or white; hood streaked purple; lip speckled pink or mauve-purple. Flowers fragrant. A large flowered form, var. *commutata* (Tod.) Richter, has longer and more attenuated sepals producing a longer hood.
Distribution, central Europe and the Mediterranean region, Asia Minor, the Crimea and the Caucasus, from sea leavel to 1500 metres. Grows in hill pastures, grassy slopes, margins of woodlands and maquis. Flowers April to June.

**Milky Orchid** *Orchis lactea* Poir.
15-30cm. Leaves six to eight, oblong-lanceolate, unspotted or rarely spotted; bracts short. Plant generally more robust than *Orchis tridentata*. Sepals very long and attenuated, forming with the petals a long whiskery-tipped hood; lip three-lobed, central lobe entire or only slightly indented. Flowers pale pink, creamy to white with or without reddish or greenish streaking; lip often unspotted.
Widespread through much of the Mediterranean region, but local: North Africa, Spain, to Greece and Lebanon. Grows in dry grassy places and amongst maquis. Flowers February to early April.

Burnt Orchid

Toothed Orchid

Milky Orchid

**Galilean Orchid** *Orchis galilaea* (Bornm. et Schulze) Schltr.
15-35cm. Leaves five to eight, lanceolate, unspotted; bracts very small, one-sixth length of ovary. Inflorescence moderately lax, cylindrical, flowers blooming from top to bottom. Sepals and petals incurved forming a hood; lip three-lobed, laterals lunate; central lobe deeply bifurcated. Flowers yellow or greenish yellow, sepals with or without red veining, lip spotted with red; spur short, about one quarter length of ovary, curved downwards.
A rather rare and local orchid found in Israel, Lebanon and Syria, growing at the edges of plantations, in olive groves and in grassy areas amongst rocks on limestone. Flowers February to early April, depending upon altitude.

**Punctate Orchid** *Orchis punctulata* Stev. ex Lindl.
25-60cm. Leaves seven to ten, broadly lanceolate, the upper leaves forming foliaceous sheaths around stem, unspotted; bracts small, about one-fifth length of ovary. Inflorescence fairly dense, cylindrical, many flowered; flowers bloom in normal sequence, opening from bottom of inflorescence to top. Sepals and petals incurved forming a loose hood; lip three-lobed, the laterals wide spreading, lunate; median lobe split deeply at apex with a short linear appendage; spur half length of ovary, down-curved. Flowers with a strong vanilla scent, yellowish-green, the sepals marked inside with purplish-brown dots; lip yellowish-green to olive green with purplish speckling.
Rare and local, recorded from Greece (rare), Cyprus, Turkey, Crimea, Caucasus, western Transcaucasia and Iran. Records from Israel and Lebanon probably refer to *Orchis galilaea*. Grows along forest margins and in forest shades, thickets and conifer woodland. Flowers March to May.

Punctate Orchid

Galilean Orchid

**Military Orchid** *Orchis militaris* L.

French *Orchis militaire* German *Helm Orchis* or *Helmkraut* Italian *Giglio-crestato*

25-60cm. Leaves seven to ten, broadly lanceolate, unspotted; bracts small, scale-like. Inflorescence moderately dense, many flowered; flower-spike at first oval, elongates during blooming. Sepals and petals incurved forming a hood; lip three-lobed, the laterals more or less curved, the median lobe divided at apex with a very small appendage in centre; spur about half length of ovary, pointing downwards. Flowers have a clear pink head, lip pale red with deeper red speckles. Widespread over most of central Europe except northern regions; rare in England; eastwards to Russia, Crimea and Caucasus. Found in undisturbed grassy areas, open woodland and thickets. Flowers from April to June.

*Orchis steveni* Rchb. is an orchid of uncertain status but closely related to *O. militaris*. Described from the Caucasus, very few specimens are known. It differs from *O. militaris* in having very much longer lobules of the median lip lobe. It is possible that it is a hybrid between *O. militaris* and *O. simia*.

**Lady Orchid** *Orchis purpurea* Hudson

French *Orchis casque* or *Orchis pourpre* German *Purpur-Orchis*

25-80cm. A very robust species. Leaves six to ten, broadly lanceolate to ovoid, shining green, unspotted; bracts up to half the length of ovary. Sepals and petals forming a rather rounded helmet; lip three-lobed, the laterals slender, median lobe very broad and rounded, indented with a small appendage in centre. Flowers, helmet reddish to blackish-brown, lip whitish to pink with purplish-red spots. Distinguished from Military Orchid by its much broader lip. England, rare, confined mainly to Kent; widespread in Europe from Denmark southwards and east to Russia; also in North Africa. Found from sea level to 700 metres in Europe, but in Mediterranean area only in mountains. Favours calcareous soils, growing in grassland, woodland, beech woods, conifer plantations and scrub. Flowers April to June.

white form

dark form

Lady Orchid

Military Orchid

**Monkey Orchid** *Orchis simia* Lam.
French *Orchis singe* German *Affen Orchis*
20-45cm. Leaves five to seven, broadly lanceolate, unspotted; bracts short, one-fifth length of ovary. Inflorescence short and relatively dense, flowers opening from top to bottom. Sepals and petals incurved forming a loose peaked helmet; lip three-lobed, laterals slender, median lobe deeply divided with a short central appendage; spur about half of length of ovary, down-pointing. Helmet silvery pink to darker red, lip white with red extremities. Distinguished from *Orchis italica* by its smoother leaves and flowering sequence.
Widespread in central and southern Europe, North Africa, eastwards to Cyprus, Israel, Lebanon, Syria and Turkey; also Crimea and Caucasus; now very rare in Britain, found only in Oxfordshire and Kent. Grows in both shady and sunny locations in grasslands, open woodlands and maquis. Flowers late March in south to early June in north.

**Naked Man Orchid** *Orchis italica* Poir.
French *Orchis ondulé* Italian *Uomo nudo*
20-40cm. Leaves seven to ten, broadly lanceolate with a wavy edge; upper leaves clasping the stem; spotted or unspotted; bracts short, one-fifth as long as ovary. Inflorescence fairly dense, oval, flowering sequence normal, from bottom to top. Sepals and petals incurved forming a peaked hood; lip elongated, three-lobed; laterals slender and pointed; median lobe deeply split and pointed, central appendage present; spur about half length of ovary, down-pointing. Hood pink to red, sometimes lightly streaked; lip white or pink with red spots. Wavy leaf edges, sequence of flowering and pointed lip lobes distinguish this species from the Monkey Orchid. A common Mediterranean species, from Portugal and Spain eastwards to Turkey and Lebanon; also North Africa. Occurs in grassy areas, open woodlands and maquis mainly on calcareous soils. Flowers March to April.

Monkey Orchid

Naked Man Orchid

**Green-Winged Orchid** *Orchis morio* L.
French *Orchis bouffon* German *Kleine Orchis* Italian *Zonzelle*
10-30cm. Leaves five to nine, lanceolate, unspotted; bracts about length of ovary, green or reddish. Inflorescence lax, five to twelve flowered. Sepals and petals incurved forming a loose, rounded hood; lip three-lobed, very broad, usually more or less folded, central lobe indented at apex; spur stubby, about length of ovary, curved upwards or horizontal. Flower colour variable, dark-purple, carmine-pink to white; lateral sepals streaked green; lip with central dark spotting.
A common and widespread species throughout Europe except in extreme north; common in British Isles. In the southern Mediterranean area, North Africa and the Middle East the nominate race is replaced by other subspecies. Grows in pastureland, open woodland and maquis on calcareous to slightly acid soils. Flowers March to June, depending upon latitude.

*Orchis morio* ssp. *picta* (Loisel.) Richter is paler and smaller flowered, 6-10mm against 12-15mm in nominate race: in Mediterranean region.

*Orchis morio* ssp. *picta* var. *libani* (Renz) Soó is a small plant, similar to *picta*, the flowers with pink to pale greenish-red hoods and a white lip without spots. Occurs in Cyprus, south-eastern Turkey and Lebanon.

*Orchis morio* ssp. *champagneuzii* (Barn.) Camus forms clumps and has a much longer and more slender spur and the lip often lacks dark spotting. Always with more than two tubers. Found in Morocco, Spain, Balearic Islands and southern France; records from Italy unconfirmed.

pale form

pale form

dark form

ssp. *picta*

pale form

ssp. *champagneuxii*

Green-winged Orchid

**Pink Butterfly Orchid** *Orchis papilionacea* L.

French *Orchis papillon* German *Schmetterling* Italian *Cipressini*

15-40cm. Stem angular; leaves six to nine, lanceolate, unspotted; bracts pink tinged, longe
than ovary. Inflorescence lax, three to eight flowered. Sepals and petals slightly incurved formin
a loose unclosed hood; lip entire, fan-shaped with toothed edge; spur about half length of ovary
curved, down-pointing. Flowers white to pink or red with darker red longitudinal streaking
Throughout the Mediterranean region as far east as Cyprus, Turkey, Lebanon and Israel; als
Bulgaria, Rumania and the Caucasus. Habitat, dry maquis, olive groves and open woodlan
on calcareous to slightly acid soils. Flowers March to May.

*Orchis papilionacea* ssp. *bruhnsiana* (Gruner) Soó has a smaller, more spatulate-shaped li
8-10mm long by 7mm wide and stumpy sepals. It occurs only in Transcaucasia.

**Long-Spurred Orchid** *Orchis longicornu* Poir.

French *Orchis à longue corne* Italian *Galetti di lungo cornu*

10-35cm. Leaves six to eight, lanceolate, unspotted; bracts about length of ovary, green c
tinged red. Inflorescence lax, five to ten flowered. Sepals and petals incurved forming a loos
helmet; lip three-lobed, the lateral lobes longer than the median lobe, recurved; spur as lon
as ovary, curved upwards and thickened at tip. Helmet pink to purplish-red, median area whi
with dark red spots.

Distribution, western Mediterranean region, North Africa, Portugal, Spain, Balearic Island
Southern France (Var), Italy, Corsica, Sardinia and Sicily. Grows in dry grasslands, ope
woods and maquis. Flowers February to April.

var.

var.

Pink Butterfly Orchid

Long-spurred Orchid

**Fan-Lipped Orchid** *Orchis saccata* Ten.
[Syn. *Orchis collina* Soland.]
French *Orchis à filtre*
10-30cm. Leaves four to six, broadly lanceolate, normally unspotted; bracts tinged purple, half the length of ovary. Inflorescence a narrow lax spike of two to fifteen flowers. Hood composed of dorsal sepal and petals, lateral sepals erect or curved backwards; lip entire, fan-shaped with wavy edge; spur short, conical, pointing downwards. Flowers deep red to purplish-red, sepals sometimes lined green.
A very uncommon and local **Mediterranean** orchid occurring from southern Spain to Turkey; also North Africa, Lebanon, Iran and the Caucasus. On limestone soils in dry grasslands, maquis and open woodland. Flowers February to April.

*Orchis saccata* ssp. *chlorotica* (Woronow)? is known only from Transcaucasia and appears to be very rare. It differs from the nominate race in having the lateral sepals forming part of the hood and the lip greenish-yellow.

**Green-Spotted Orchid** *Orchis patens* Desf.
French *Orchis étalé*
20-45cm. Leaves five to eight, broadly lanceolate to linear, spotted or unspotted; bracts as long as ovary. Inflorescence lax, up to thirty flowered. Dorsal sepal and petals curved inwards, lateral sepals erect or sometimes horizontal; lip three-lobed, median lobe slightly indented; spur conical, down-pointing, about half length of ovary. Flowers, lateral sepals pale red with a large green spot; lip pink with dark red speckles.
A very rare species most frequent in the mountains of Algeria: also recorded Tunisia, southern Spain, Balearic Islands, northern Italy and Crete. Grows in mountain meadows up to 1600 metres, in open woodland and amongst maquis thickets, on limestone. Flowers March to May.

**Spitzel's Orchid** *Orchis spitzelii* Sauter ex Koch
[Syn. *Orchis viridifusca* Alboff]
French *Orchis de Spitzel* or *Orchis à corne courte* German *Spitzels Knabenkraut*
20-50cm. Leaves seven to eight, lanceolate, unspotted; bracts about as long as ovary. Inflorescence, a loose spike, five to eighteen flowered. Dorsal sepal and petals slightly incurved forming an open hood; lateral sepals incurving or moderately erect; lip three-lobed, median lobe slightly indented; spur slightly shorter than ovary, conical, down-pointing. Sepals greenish-brown to green on inner surface, dotted with red; lip pink to dark red with dark red spots. Closely related to *O. patens* but differs in colour of sepals and length of spur.
Algeria, Spain, France (Alps), Austria, Italy in southern Alps, Yugoslavia, Greece, Turkey, Crimea and Caucasus. A relict species, rare and extremely local. Grows in mountain meadows up to 1800 metres. Flowers April to July according to altitude.

lip and spur

Spitzel's Orchid

lateral lobes often folded under median lobe

Green-Spotted Orchid

reen-lipped form

pink-lipped form

Fan-lipped Orchid

**Canary Islands Orchid** *Orchis canariensis* Ldl.
15-35cm. Leaves five to seven, lanceolate, unspotted; bracts slightly longer than ovary. Inflorescence fairly lax, ten to twenty flowered. Dorsal sepal and petals slightly incurved to form an open hood; laterals spreading or erect; lip three-lobed; spur conical, pointing more or less upwards, about half length of ovary. Flowers pinkish-white to pink with red spots; sepals often greenish on inner surface.
Endemic to the Canary Islands. Grows in ravines and amongst thickets in undisturbed ground, from 800 to 1400 metres, in slightly acid soil. Flowers February and March.

**Anatolian Orchid** *Orchis anatolica* Boiss.
10-25cm. Leaves five to eight, lanceolate, spotted; bracts short, less than half length of ovary. Inflorescence lax, five to eight flowered. Dorsal sepal and petals incurved forming loose hood; laterals erect; lip three lobed; spur cylindrical, very long and slender, horizontal or pointing upwards. Flowers pale rosy-purple with sparse red spotting at base of lip.
Eastern Mediterranean, Cyclades and Aegean Islands, Turkey south to Israel. Also reported to occur in Tunisia. Habitat, grassy slopes and amongst open bush. Flowers March and April.

**Four-Spotted Orchid** *Orchis quadripunctata* Cyr.
15-25cm. Slender habit, leaves six to eight, lanceolate, spotted or unspotted. Inflorescence an elongated lax spike of eight to twenty flowers. Dorsal sepal more or less erect, petals incurved, lateral sepals spreading; lip rectangular, three-lobed; spur long and slender, down-pointing. Flowers pink to violet-pink, the lip base with two or four small dark purple spots. Differs from *O. boryi* in flowering from bottom upwards. Distribution, an uncommon and local species known from Italy to Turkey, Sardinia and Cyprus. Habitat stony hillside with sparse grass. Flowers April and May.

**Bory's Orchid** *Orchis boryi* Rehb.
15-35cm. Leaves five to seven, slender, lanceolate, unspotted; bracts slightly shorter than ovary. Inflorescence short and three to six flowered, blooming from top of inflorescence downwards. Sepals slightly incurved forming a loose hood; lip three-lobed but sometimes side lobes poorly defined; spur long and slender, horizontal or down-pointing. Flowers deep violet-red, paler on the lip which is marked with two or four dark red spots. Flowering sequence distinguishes *O. boryi* from similar Four-Spotted Orchid.
Rare and little known, recorded from Greece and Crete. Grows in open maquis and thickets on limestone. Flowers during April.

Bory's Orchid

white form

Canary Islands Orchid

Four-Spotted Orchid

Anatolian Orchid

**Early Purple Orchid** *Orchis mascula* L.
French *Orchis mâle* German *Männliche Orchis* Italian *Giglio-caprino*
30-55cm. Leaves seven to eleven, broadly lanceolate, green with deep purplish spots, rarely unspotted; bracts shorter than ovary, tinged purple. Inflorescence lax, six to twenty flowered. Dorsal sepal and petals incurved forming a rounded hood; lateral sepals spreading or reflexed; lip three-lobed, median lobe notched; spur stout, about as long as ovary, horizontal or upward-pointing. Flowers mauve-red to purplish-crimson, lip whitish in centre with deep red spots. Flowers have a strong odour of cat urine.
A common species over most of Europe including Britain, eastwards to Turkey, Russia and the Caucasus. Grows up to 2500 metres; favours open woodlands, moist pastures and thickets on clay soils. Flowers April to July. Several distinct races are recognized.

*Orchis mascula* ssp. *olbiensis* (Reuter ex Greiner) A. et G. is a slender form from the western Mediterranean area—Spain, France, Corsica, the Balearic Islands, Morocco and Algeria. 10-25cm. Leaves lanceolate, usually unspotted; bracts very short. Inflorescence lax, five to fifteen flowered. Lateral sepals erect. Flowers pink or mauve-pink, the lip whitish, purple spotted in centre; spur longer than the ovary and up-pointing. Lacks the 'tom cat' smell of the nominate race.

*Orchis mascula* ssp. *signifera* (Vest) Soó has the spike dense, many flowered; the sepals are long, acuminate, forming a spiked apex to the hood; lip, median lobe up to twice as long as laterals. Occurs in central, southern and eastern Europe.

*Orchis mascula* ssp. *wanikowii* (Wulff) Soó has a very lax, few flowered inflorescence, the sepals are lilac veined purplish-brown and the central lobe of the lip is one and a half times the length of the lateral lobes. Known only from the Crimea.

ssp. *signifera*

ssp. *olbiensis*

Early Purple Orchid

**Pale-Flowered Orchid** *Orchis pallens* L.
French *Orchis pâle* German *Blasse Orchis*
10-30cm. Leaves seven to nine, broadly lanceolate, unspotted; bracts about same length as ovary. Inflorescence dense. Dorsal sepal and petals incurved forming a loose hood; lateral sepals erect; lip three-lobed, unspotted; spur stout, slightly shorter than ovary, horizontal or upwards-pointing. Flowers elder-scented, yellow or less frequently rose-red, the sepals and petals paler than the lip. The similar Elder-flowered Orchid has a down-pointing spur.
A mountain pasture and woodland orchid, widespread in central and southern Europe to Turkey, Lebanon and eastwards to the Caucasus. Flowers April to June.

**Provence Orchid** *Orchis provincialis* Balb.
French *Orchis de Provence* German *Provenzalische Orchis*
20-30cm. A rather slender plant with seven to nine broadly lanceolate leaves, usually spotted; bracts narrow, as long as ovary. Inflorescence lax to rather dense, seven to twenty flowered. Dorsal sepal erect, laterals spreading, petals incurved to form incomplete hood; lip three-lobed; spur slightly longer than ovary, curved and pointing upwards. Flowers yellow; lip has a central orange-yellow patch with purplish-red spots.
A Mediterranean species locally common in parts of southern Europe and North Africa, favouring grassy slopes, open woodland and thickets on calcareous soils. Flowers April to June.

**Sparse-Flowered Orchid** *Orchis provincialis* ssp. *pauciflora* (Ten.) Camus
French *Orchis à fleurs peu nombreuses*
10-30cm. Leaves seven to nine, broadly lanceolate, unspotted to rarely sparsely spotted; bracts shorter than ovary. Inflorescence lax, few flowered, usually from three to seven. Sepals erect or recurved; petals incurved forming an uncomplete hood; lip three-lobed, median lobe indented; spur longer than ovary, curved and pointing upwards. Flowers yellow, rarely rose-red, the lip brighter with an orange centre speckled with red-brown.
A very uncommon eastern subspecies known from Italy, Yugoslavia, Corsica, Greece, Crete and Asia Minor. Habitat, woodlands and semi-shady grassy slopes. Flowers April to June.

Pale-Flowered Orchid     Provence Orchid     Sparse-Flowered Orchid

**Loose-Flowered Orchid** *Orchis laxiflora* Lam.
French *Orchis à fleurs lâches* German *Lockerblütige Orchis*
30-50cm. Leaves seven to ten, lanceolate, channelled, unspotted; bracts shorter than ovary, tinged purple. Inflorescence lax, six to twenty flowered. Sepals outspread, petals incurved forming loose hood; lip slightly three-lobed, the lateral lobes longer than the central lobe; spur normally half the length of ovary, sometimes longer, horizontal or slightly up-curved; widened at tip. Flowers claret-red, violet, pink or rarely white. The race *palustris* has the lip distinctly three-lobed and the central lobe longer than the laterals.
Mainly a Mediterranean species, extending eastwards to Turkey, Syria and Iraq; also occurs in North Africa and found in the Channel Islands. Grows in marshes, boggy meadows and damp sandy places. Flowers May and June.

*Orchis laxiflora* ssp. *palustris* (Jacq.) A. et G. is sometimes considered a distinct species. Differs from the nominate race in having the lip deeply three-lobed, median lobe at least as long as the laterals, normally longer; the spur not widened at tip. Occurs mainly in northern and southern parts of species' range.

*Orchis laxiflora* ssp. *palustris* var. *elegans* (Heuffel) Beck has a slightly longer lip which is subentire or shallowly three-lobed, with the central lobe as long as the laterals.
Found in east-central Europe.

oose-Flowered
Orchid

ssp. *palustris*

## Komper's Orchid *Comperia*

Perennial. 15-45(55)cm. Tubers two, ovoid or ellipsoid, undivided. Two or three oblong-lanceolate leaves at base of stem and green sheathing leaves above. Inflorescence erect, rather loosely three to ten flowered (up to 25 flowers on exceptional plants). Perianth, sepals fused for three-quarters of length, curved inwards forming a hood with the petals; lip three-lobed, the lateral lobes and the bifurcated central lobe prolonged into very long filiform appendages; bracts membranous. *Comperia* is a monotypic genus, the single species with a restricted eastern distribution.

### Komper's Orchid *Comperia comperiana* (Steven) Asch. & Graeb.

15-55cm. Leaves at base two to three, lanceolate, unspotted, with sheathing leaves above; bracts about same length as ovary. Inflorescence cylindrical, lax to fairly dense. Sepals and petals incurved forming a hood, the former reflexed at tips; petals lanceolate with one or two long teeth on each side; lip three-lobed, the median lobe split into two, all four divisions greatly lengthened into very slender filiform processes; spur cylindrical, shorter than ovary, pointing downwards. Hood brownish- or greenish-purple; lip whitish, pale pink or pale red. This is one of the great rarities amongst European orchids, known from the Crimea, the islands of Lesbos and Samos, Turkey, Lebanon and Iran. Grows in conifer forests mainly between 500 and 2000 metres on limestone soils. Flowers April to August, depending on altitude.

## Hooded Orchid *Steveniella*

Perennial. 15-35cm. Tubers two, ellipsoid, undivided. A solitary more or less lanceolate leaf a little above the base, followed by two foliaceous sheaths. Inflorescence erect, fairly densely seven to twenty flowered. Perianth, sepals fused into an oval hood, three-toothed at apex; petals free; lip broadly three-lobed, rounded and thick at apex; spur short, 2mm long; bracts half length of ovary, membranous. The single species is local and rare with a restricted eastern distribution.

### Hooded Orchid *Steveniella satyrioides* (Steven) Schlech.

15-35cm. A single lanceolate leaf near the base and two sheathing leaves above; leaf normally tinted reddish; bracts shorter than ovary. Inflorescence lax to fairly dense, seven to twenty flowered. Sepals fused into an oval hood, attenuated at apex; petals very short, free; lip three-lobed, the median lobe rounded, entire, longer than side lobes; spur short, conical, pointing downwards. Flowers variable in colour, dull green, yellowish-green or reddish-brown, base of lip purplish-brown.

This is another orchid of extreme rarity, known from the Crimea and Pontus in eastern Turkey where it occurs in mountain pastures and open woodlands. Flowers April to May.

Komper's Orchid          Hooded Orchid

# Marsh and Spotted Orchids *Dactylorhiza*

Perennials. 10-50(80)cm. Tubers normally two, palmately lobed or divided. Leaves four to many, normally linear-lanceolate, spotted or unspotted; bracts leaf-like, often longer than the flowers. Lateral sepals erect, spreading or reflexed, rarely incurved; lip spreading or slightly recurved, entire to three-lobed; spur present. The genus *Dactylorhiza* differs from *Orchis* in the palmate tubers and the leaf-like bracts which are normally longer than the flowers. Approximately 18 species occur in Europe, some of which are widespread and locally abundant. Classification and status of several is controversial. The *Dactylorhiza* species readily hybridize with each other and individual plants and colonies may be difficult to identify.

**Crimean Orchid** *Dactylorhiza iberica* (Bieb.) Soó [Syn. *Orchis iberica* Bieb.]
20-40cm. Leaves five to seven, linear-lanceolate, unspotted; bracts narrow, usually longer than ovary. Inflorescence lax, six to ten flowered, sepals and petals incurved forming a helmet; lip three-lobed, rarely entire, median lobe more slender than laterals; spur cylindrical, curved, half length of ovary. Flowers pink, lip spotted purple or magenta; spur white towards base. A very distinct species easily recognized by its incurved sepals and petals.
Mountain regions, over 800 metres, of northern Greece, Crimea, Cyprus, Turkey, Lebanon, Caucasus and Iran. Grows in marshes and seepages, flowering from May to August.

**Elder-Flowered Orchid** *Dactylorhiza sambucina* (L.) Soó [Syn. *Orchis sambucina* L.]
French *Orchis sureau* German *Hollunder Orchis* Italian *Giglio sambucino*
The species is inaptly named as it has very little scent: it is the somewhat similar *Orchis pallens* that has a strong elder scent.
10-30cm. Leaves four to five, broadly lanceolate, unspotted; bracts slender, longer than ovary. Inflorescence dense, many flowered. Lateral sepals recurved; dorsal sepal and petals incurved; lip shallowly three lobed; spur about as long as ovary, down-pointing. Flowers pale yellow or less commonly magenta; rarely bicoloured. The closely related *D. romana* has more leaves and the spur is horizontal or pointing up.
Widespread over much of Europe from southern Scandinavia southwards, North Africa and the Near East, but absent from many Mediterranean islands and most of Russia. Grows in mountain pastures from 500 to 2000 metres, often in large colonies. Flowers between March and June.

*Dactylorhiza sambucina* ssp. *insularis* (Somm.) Soó is endemic to Corsica and Sardinia; it has a lax inflorescence and a shorter spur.

**Roman Orchid** *Dactylorhiza romana* (Seb. & Mauri) Soó
[Syn. *Orchis romana* Seb. et Mauri]
Italian *Giglio bratteoso*
20-45cm. Leaves eight to twelve, lanceolate, unspotted; bracts longer than ovary. Inflorescence lax, seven or more flowered. Sepals erect, petals incurved; lip three-lobed, central lobe square; spur longer than ovary, up-curved or horizontal. Flowers yellow or magenta.
Southern Europe and North Africa eastwards to Cyprus, Turkey, Crimea and Iran. On bushy or stone slopes, in maquis and lower mountain pastures up to 1800 metres. Flowers March to June.

*Dactylorhiza romana* ssp. *siciliensis* (Klinge) Soó has a shorter, more conical spur.
From south-western Spain, southern Italy, Sicily and Sardinia.

*Dactylorhiza romana* ssp. *bartonii* Huxley & Hunt has an orange-red patch at the base of the lip. From Portugal

Crimean Orchid

ssp. *bartonii*

pink form

pink form

Elder-Flowered Orchid                    Roman Orchid

**Early Marsh Orchid** *Dactylorhiza incarnata*
(L.) Soó
French *Orchis incarnat* German *Fleischfarbige
Ragwurz*
15-80cm, stem hollow. Leaves four to seven,
slender to broad lanceolate, unspotted; acuminate, often hooded at tip; yellowish-green; bracts
longer than ovary. Inflorescence dense, many
flowered. Lateral sepals spreading, recurved;
lip small, entire or shallowly three-lobed with
small central tooth, sides of lip folded back; spur
straight, shorter than ovary, down-pointing.
Flowers variable from white to pink or lilac.
Var. *ochroleuca* (Boll.) Hunt & Summerhayes
with yellowish-white flowers occurs sporadically
through range.
Most of Europe but rare in Mediterranean area;
North Africa, northern Turkey to Caucasus.
Habitat, damp grasslands, dune slacks, fens and
bogs. Flowers April to July.
*D. incarnata* frequently hybridizes with other
closely related species; many plants and often
thriving colonies are found which are extremely
difficult to identify with accuracy. Some of these
populations have received names of uncertain
status.

*Dactylorhiza incarnata* ssp. *coccinea* (Pugsley)
Soó has crimson-red flowers and erect, normally
hooded, unspotted leaves.
Found in Britain and Ireland; unconfirmed
record from Netherlands. Generally grows in
damp sand-dune slacks.

*Dactylorhiza incarnata* ssp. *pulchella* (Druce)
Soó, also from Britain and Ireland, has purple
flowers frequently streaked with red.

*Dactylorhiza incarnata* ssp. *cruenta* (Müller)
D. M. Moore & Soó is 18-30cm tall and has
leaves heavily spotted with violet on both
surfaces; flowers crimson or purplish-red. From
northern and eastern Europe and the Alps.

ssp. *cruenta*

Early Marsh Orchid

ssp. *coccinea*

var. *ochroleuca*

**Robust Marsh Orchid** *Dactylorhiza elata*
(Poiret) Soó [Syn. *Orchis elata* Poiret]
30-110cm, stem narrowly hollow. Leaves eight
to fourteen, broadly lanceolate, unspotted, the
uppermost bract-like; bracts longer than ovary.
Inflorescence usually dense, many flowered.
Outer sepals spreading, reflexed; lip broader
than long, subentire to three-lobed; lateral lobes
often reflexed; spur cylindrical, decurved.
Flowers pink to purplish-red. Distinguished
from *D. incarnata* by broad lip.
South-western Europe eastwards to Sicily;
North Africa; grows in wet meadows, bogs and
seepages. Flowers April to end of June.

**Broad-Leaved Marsh Orchid** *Dactylorhiza
majalis* (Rchb.) Hunt et Summerh. [Syn. *Orchis
majalis* Rchb.]
French *Orchis à larges feuilles* German *Breit-
blattrige Knabenkraut*
20-60cm, stem hollow. Leaves four to eight,
broadly lanceolate, usually widest in the middle,
normally with heavy purple spotting on the
upper side; bracts much longer than ovary.
Inflorescence dense, many flowered. Outer
sepals spreading or reflexed; lip three-lobed,
centre of median lobe without markings; spur
half length of ovary, pendent. Flowers deep
magenta to purplish-lilac.
Western and central Europe, northwards to
Finland and eastwards to Russia. This is the
commonest Marsh Orchid in central Europe,
growing in swamps and marshy ground. Flowers
May to July. An extremely variable species.

*Dactylorhiza majalis* ssp. *occidentalis* (Pugsley)
D. M. Moore et Soó
[Syn. *D. kerryensis* (Wilmott) H. & S.]
10-25cm. Leaves broadly lanceolate, widest in
middle, with large or irregular spots. Lip three-
lobed or subentire; median lobe with broken
line markings.
Britain and Ireland. Flowers April to May.

*Dactylorhiza majalis* ssp. *alpestris* (Pugsley)
Senghas
15-30cm. Has lower leaves elliptical, widest
towards apex, with large or irregular spots.
Flowers purplish-lilac to deep magenta, lip
usually subentire, rarely three-lobed, median
lobe without markings. Recorded from the Alps
and Pyrenees. Flowers July to August.

Robust Marsh Orchid

Broad-Leaved Marsh Orchid

ssp. *occidentalis*

**Southern Marsh Orchid** *Dactylorhiza prae-termissa* (Druce) Soó
20-75cm. Leaves five to seven, lanceolate, widest below middle, unspotted. Flowers pale pinkish-red to rose-purple; lip shallowly three-lobed, median lobe with red speckling.
North-western Europe, including Britain. Flowers mid-June to July.

**Northern Marsh Orchid** *Dactylorhiza pur-purella* (T. et T. A. Steph.) Soó
20-45cm. Leaves five to eight, lanceolate, widest below middle, normally unspotted but some-times sparsely spotted towards apex. Lip sub-entire or rarely shallowly three-lobed with dark lines and spots; flowers magenta.
North-western Europe including northern parts of British Isles. Flowers late June to early August.

*Dactylorhiza baltica* (Klinge) Orlova from northern and eastern Europe is of uncertain status; described as similar to *D.m. purpurella* but with narrower leaves and lip three-lobed.

**Scandinavian Marsh Orchid** *Dactylorhiza pseudocordigera* (Neuman) Soó
8-20cm. Leaves three to four, spreading or erect, elliptical to lanceolate with dense dark spots; lip 6-7mm long; spur conical, half as long as ovary. Flowers purplish-red with darker mark-ings.
Norway and Sweden, growing in marshes and damp pastures. Flowers July and August.

Scandinavian Marsh Orchid

Northern Marsh Orchid

Southern
Marsh Orchid

**Heart-Shaped Orchid** *Dactylorhiza cordigera* (Fries) Soó
15-30cm. Leaves two to five, lanceolate to oblong, spreading, normally spotted purplish-brown on both surfaces; bracts longer than ovary. Inflorescence lax, to moderately dense. Lateral sepals erect; lip entire, very broad, heart-shaped; spur pendant, half length of ovary. Flowers deep rose-red to magenta with line markings.
Restricted to south-eastern Europe—southern Yugoslavia, Bulgaria, Rumania, Greece and western Russia, growing in marshy places in mountains from 1000 to 2400 metres. Flowers July and August.

*Dactylorhiza cordigera* ssp. *bosniaca* (Beck) Soó has a long stem and the inflorescence dense; lip square, wedge-shaped at base. From Albania, Yugoslavia and Bulgaria.

*Dactylorhiza cordigera* ssp. *siculorum* (Soó) Soó is similar to *D.c. bosniaca* but has lanceolate petals and a more or less circular lip, entire or deeply three-lobed. From Rumania to western Russia.

**Pugsley's Marsh Orchid** *Dactylorhiza traunsteineri* (Sauter) Soó
French *Orchis de Traunsteiner* German *Traunsteiners Orchis*
15-45cm. Leaves four to seven, lanceolate, normally erect, spotted or unspotted; bracts longer than ovary. Inflorescence rather lax, few to many flowered. Sepals oblong-lanceolate, laterals spreading or reflexed; lip subentire or shallowly three-lobed with deflexed margin; median lobe distinctly longer than side lobes; spur half as long as ovary, pendent. Flowers magenta marked with dark purple-red.
Northern and central Europe, the following race being dominant in the northern region. Grows in marshes and bogs in acid soil, often amongst sphagnum moss. Flowers late June to August.

*Dactylorhiza traunsteineri* ssp. *curvifolia* (Nyl.) Soó has two to four spreading, strongly curved leaves which are keeled on upper surface; lip shallowly three-lobed, median lobe only slightly longer than laterals. Flowers pale magenta with darker markings on lip.
From Sweden, Finland and northern Russia.

*Dactylorhiza russowii* (Klinge) Holub is of uncertain and controversial status. It is described as being similar to nominate *D. traunsteineri* but has a dense inflorescence; flowers pink; lip flat, the central lobe triangular; spur slightly shorter than ovary. From eastern and east-central Europe.

**Anatolian Marsh Orchid** *Dactylorhiza cilicica* (Klinge) P. F. Hunt et Summerh.
30-75cm. Leaves six or seven, lanceolate to broadly lanceolate, usually erect, unspotted; bracts longer than the flowers, tinged purplish-brown. Inflorescence dense; lateral sepals spreading; lip entire, rounded, lengthened at apex; spur shorter than ovary, thick, pointed downwards. Flowers mauve with darker markings.
Turkey, in the mountains of central Anatolia and eastern Taurus, growing in wet alpine pasture. Flowers May to July.

Anatolian
Marsh Orchid

Pugsley's Marsh Orchid

Heart-Shaped Orchid

**Madeiran Orchid** *Dactylorhiza foliosa* (Sol. ex Lowe) Soó
40-60cm. Leaves four to five, lanceolate, unspotted; bracts longer than ovary. Inflorescence fairly dense, many flowered. Lateral sepals slightly incurved; lip broader than long, three-lobed; spur slender, about half as long as ovary. Flowers pink, the lip with indistinct spotting.
Endemic to Madeira where it grows in marshy pastures. Flowers May to June.

**Wedge-Lipped Orchid** *Dactylorhiza saccifera* (Brong.) Soó
French *Orchis à sac*
30-50cm. Leaves five to eight, broadly lanceolate to elliptical, unspotted; bracts very long, protruding out of inflorescence. Inflorescence fairly lax, few to many flowered. Lateral sepals spreading; lip deeply three-lobed, acuminate, side lobes more or less deeply toothed; spur thick, as long as ovary. Flowers pink with dark red markings.
Southern Europe from Spain eastwards to Greece and the Balkans; uncertainly North Africa. Restricted to subalpine and alpine zone to 2500 metres, growing in wet mountain pastures and in open woodland. Flowers May to July.

**Caucasian Marsh Orchid** *Dactylorhiza cata-onica* (Fleischm.) Holub
[Syn. *Orchis caucasica* (Klinge) Medvyedev]
10-30cm. Leaves few, erect or horizontal, spotted; bracts longer than ovary. Inflorescence lax, few flowered. Sepals spreading; lip very broad, entire, rarely three-lobed; spur thick, about two-thirds length of ovary. Flowers dark red to magenta with darker red markings. Somewhat similar to *D. cordigera* but occurs outside the range of that plant.
Eastern Turkey (Pontus) to Armenia and the Caucasus, growing in moist mountain pastures up to 2500 metres. Flowers June to July.

Caucasian Marsh Orchid

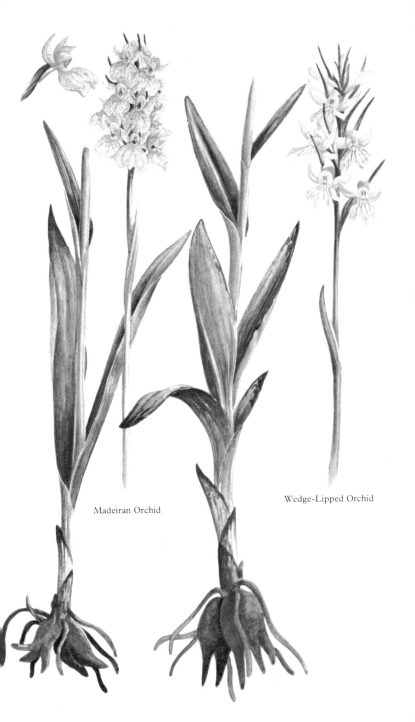

Madeiran Orchid

Wedge-Lipped Orchid

**Lapland Marsh Orchid** *Dactylorhiza lapponica* (Laest. ex Hartm.) Soó
10-20cm. Leaves two to four, lanceolate, upper bract-like, spotted or unspotted; bracts about as long as ovary. Inflorescence lax, few flowered. Sepals spreading; lip indistinctly three-lobed; spur conical, two-thirds length of ovary. Flowers mauve to reddish with darker markings.
N. Scandinavia and N. Russia, in sphagnum bogs. Flowers July to August.

**Common Spotted Orchid** *Dactylorhiza fuchsii* (Druce) Soó
French *Orchis tacheté* German *Gefleckte Orchis* Italian *Concordia*
20-60cm, stem solid. Leaves seven to twelve, erect to spreading, broad, heavily spotted; lowest leaf stumpy; bracts longer than ovary. Inflorescence dense, usually many flowered. Sepals spreading; lip deeply three-lobed, the median lobe elongated, acuminate; spur shorter than ovary, down-pointing. Flowers pale pink, mauve or white with deep red or purplish dots and lines. Variable, many forms have been described. Typical *D. fuchsii* differs from typical examples of *D. maculata* in having the middle lobe of the lip elongated and acuminate; in *D. maculata* the lip is broader with the middle lobe small and triangular.
Throughout most of Europe except the south. Grows mainly on calcareous soils in grassland, open scrub and woodland margins. Flowers June to August.

*Dactylorhiza fuchsii* ssp. *psychrophila* (Schltr.) Holub is smaller, up to 25cm with one or two leaves; flowers pink to reddish-purple. From central Europe to Scandinavia.

*Dactylorhiza fuchsii* ssp. *sooiana* (Borsos) Borsos has a stem up to 60cm; leaves up to twelve, erect or spreading; flowers white, streaked or spotted with purple. From Hungary.

**Heath Spotted Orchid** *Dactylorhiza maculata* (L.) Soó
15-60cm, stem solid. Leaves five to twelve, lanceolate, usually spotted; bracts as long as or rarely longer than flowers. Inflorescence dense, few to many flowered. Sepals horizontal or recurved; lip very broad, three-lobed, central lobe small, triangular, shorter to as long as lateral lobes; spur three-quarters length of ovary. Flowers variable, pink, mauve, reddish or white with darker markings. An extremely variable species, and identification is often further confused by plants of hybrid origin.
Most of Europe including Russia, except the south-eastern countries; North Africa uncertain. Grows in acid soils, heaths, moorlands, bogs and lightly wooded areas. Flowers late April to August. Numerous populations have been described, including the following:

*Dactylorhiza maculata* ssp. *transsilvanica* (Schur) Soó with a yellowish-white lip and unspotted leaves; from Yugoslavia and Eastern Carpathians.

*Dactylorhiza maculata* ssp. *elodes* (Griseb.) Soó has leaves with or without spots; lip pink, pale lilac or reddish; median lobe usually shorter to as long as laterals. Peat moorlands, over most of range of nominate race.

*Dactylorhiza maculata* ssp. *ericetorum* (Linton) P. F. Hunt et Summerh. is a weakly differentiated subspecies, distinguished from *D.m.* ssp. *elodes* only by its slightly longer spur, shorter than ovary (half length of ovary in *elodes*), and usually more leafy stem with 5-12 cauline leaves (4-6 in *elodes*). Peat moorlands and heaths in Britain, Ireland, Sweden and Holland: common.

*Dactylorhiza maculata* ssp. *schurii* (Klinge) Soó is similar to *elodes*, has leaves sparsely spotted; median lobe of lip as long as or longer than lateral lobes. From the Carpathians.

*Dactylorhiza maculata* ssp. *islandica* (Löve) Soó is small, 10-20cm, with a hollow stem; leaves unspotted; lip pink, pale lilac or reddish, central lobe as long as laterals; spur shorter than ovary. From Iceland.

*Dactylorhiza maculata* ssp. *lancibracteata* (C. Koch) Soó has very long green bracts spotted with purple; flowers pale mauve-lilac. Pontic Mountains, eastern Turkey and the Caucasus.

Lapland
Marsh Orchid

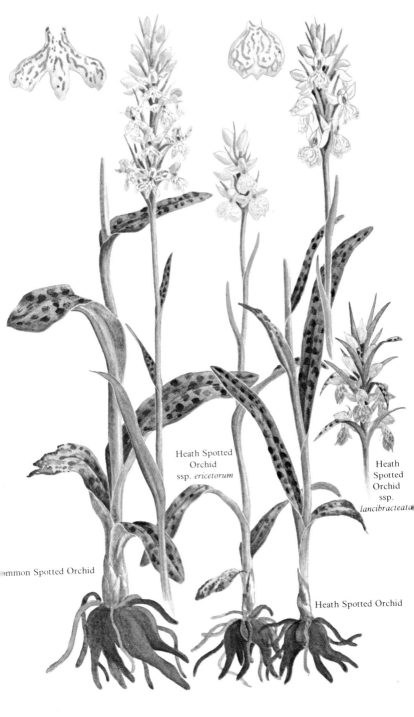

Heath Spotted
Orchid
ssp. *ericetorum*

Heath
Spotted
Orchid
ssp.
*lancibracteata*

ommon Spotted Orchid

Heath Spotted Orchid

# Globe Orchid *Traunsteinera*

Perennial. 20-45(65)cm. Tubers two, undivided. Base of stem with sheaths, the leaves arising from centre of stem; inflorescence a pyramidal cone with flowers densely packed; bracts membranous; perianth segments spreading, with spatulate tips; lip deeply three-lobed; spur about half length of ovary, down-pointing. Three-lobed rostellum, median lobe erect. This is a mountain orchid, the single species widely distributed between 1000 and 3000 metres.

**Globe Orchid** *Traunsteinera globosa* (L.) Reichenb.
French *Orchis globuleux* German *Kugelförmige Orchis*
15-65cm. Leaves two to three, oblong-lanceolate with bract-like leaves above; bracts equalling or longer than ovary. Inflorescence dense, globose, lengthening as flowers open. Sepals spreading, with spatulate tips; lip deeply three-lobed, median lobe oblong, sometimes dentate; spur half length of ovary or shorter, down-pointing. Flowers pinkish-lilac, petals and lip with purple spots. Widespread in European mountains, in the Alps, Jura, Vosges, Pyrenees, Carpathians and Balkans, east to Turkey, Russia and Caucasus. Grows in limestone mountain meadows and woodlands from 1000 to 3000 metres. Flowers May to August depending upon altitude.

*Traunsteinera globosa* ssp. *sphaerica* (M. Bieb.) Soo from the Caucasus and Transcaucasia, has flowers white speckled with purple and the central lobe of the lip attenuated to a spatulate tip.

# Dwarf Alpine Orchid *Chamorchis*

Perennial. 6-12cm. Tubers two, ovoid, undivided. Leaves all basal, slender, grooved and grass-like, often exceeding the flowering stem in length. Stem leafless with loose, few flowered spike. Sepals and petals incurved forming a hood; lip variable, entire or with very small side lobes at base; no spur; bracts longer than flowers. The single species is very difficult to find on account of its grass-like leaves and insignificant flower spike.

**Dwarf Alpine Orchid** *Chamorchis alpina* (L.) L. C. M. Richard
French *Orchis des Alpes* German *Zwergorchis* Italian *Testicolo Gramignole*
6-12cm. Leaves four to eight, all arising from base, linear, erect; bracts slender, longer than flowers. Inflorescence lax, few flowered. Sepals and petals incurved forming a hood; lip entire or shallowly three-lobed; no spur. Flowers greenish-yellow, variably tinged purplish. Widespread in mountains of Europe from Scandinavia, the Alps and Carpathians eastwards to Russia. In damp mountain pastures on limestone. Flowers July to August.

# Black Vanilla Orchid *Nigritella*

Perennial. 8-25cm. Tubers two, oval, palmate. Leaves numerous, narrow. Stem triangular, inflorescence dense, conical, later elongating; bracts slender, as long as flowers. Sepals lance shaped, spreading; lip entire, triangular, directed upwards; spur small and blunt; ovary not twisted. Rostellum small. Flowers vanilla scented. A species confined to alpine meadows.

**Black Vanilla Orchid** *Nigritella nigra* (L.) Rchb. [Syn. *N. miniata* (Crantz) Janchen]
French *Nigritelle noire* German *Schwarze Männertreu* Italian *Christi fragantissima*
8-25cm. Leaves numerous, slender, channelled; bracts longer than ovary. Inflorescence a dense many flowered conical spike, later elongating as flowers open. Sepals spreading; lip entire to indistinctly lobed, pointing upwards; spur shorter than ovary. Flowers blackish-crimson, rarely red, yellowish or white; vanilla scented.
An orchid of high mountain pastures and woods from 1000 to 2800 metres, from Scandinavia through Europe to the Balkans and Greece. Flowers June to August.

*Nigritella nigra* ssp. *ruba* (Wettst.) Camus has the inflorescence more or less cylindrical and flowers red; petals almost as wide as the sepals.
Uncommon and local in the central and eastern Alps and Rumanian mountains. Flowers earlier than nominate race, from late May.

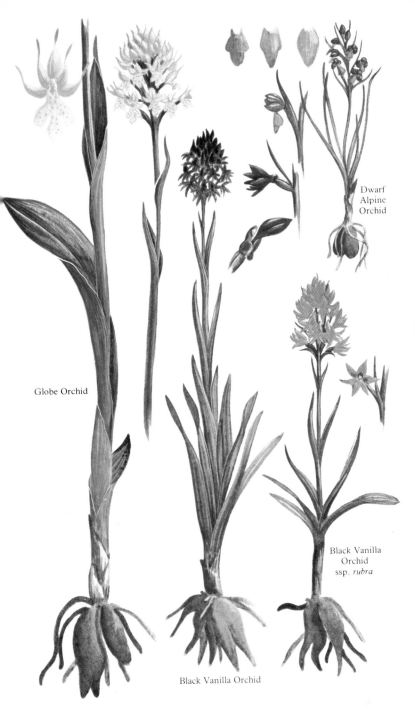

Globe Orchid

Dwarf
Alpine
Orchid

Black Vanilla
Orchid
ssp. *rubra*

Black Vanilla Orchid

# Fragrant Orchids *Gymnadenia*

Perennials. 15-45cm. Tubers two, palmate. Leaves linear-lanceolate, unspotted. Flower spike dense. Lateral sepals spreading, dorsal sepal incurved forming a hood with the petals; lip three-lobed; spur either very long and slender *(G. conopsea)* or a little shorter than the ovary *(G. odoratissima)*. Rostellum fairly long. Two species found in Europe, growing in grassland, marshes and woodland margins. Sweet scented.

**Fragrant Orchid** *Gymnadenia conopsea* (L.) R. Br.
French *Orchis moustique* German *Mücken Handwurz* Italian *Orchide garofanata*
15-45cm. Leaves four to eight, linear-lanceolate, erect, keeled, unspotted; bracts at least as long as ovary. Inflorescence dense, many flowered. Side sepals spreading, horizontal, dorsal sepal and petals incurved to form a hood; lip three-lobed, lobes subequal and rounded; spur long and slender, to twice length of ovary, projecting downwards. Flowers pink to reddish-lilac, rarely magenta or white; fragrant.

Found locally over much of Europe including British Isles, north to Scandinavia, but absent from certain areas in the south-west and south-east; occurs eastwards to Turkey, Iran, Russia, Crimea and Caucasus. Outside European region to Siberia, northern China and Japan. Grows in a variety of habitats from grassland or calcareous soils and high mountain pastures to marshy places, moorland and open woodlands. Flowers May to August depending upon latitude and altitude. Plants in wet areas often have an extremely robust growth and have been named var. *densiflora* Lindl.

**Short-Spurred Fragrant Orchid** *Gymnadenia odoratissima* (L.) L. C. M. Richard
French *Gymnadenia odorant* German *Wohlreichende Handwurz*
15-30cm. Leaves four to six, linear, erect, keeled, unspotted; bracts as long as ovary. Inflorescence dense, many flowered; flowers similar to those of *G. conopsea* but spur much shorter, not longer than ovary; flowers pale pink to white, fragrant.
Central Europe northwards to southern Sweden, south to northern Spain, north Italy and Yugoslavia, eastwards to west-central Russia. Habitat, grasslands, mountain pastures up to 2500 metres and open conifer woodlands on calcareous soils. Flowers May to August.

Fragrant Orchid

Fragrant Orchid
var. *densiflora*

Short-Spurred
Fragrant Orchid

# White Frog Orchids *Leucorchis*

Perennials. 10-30cm. Tubers two, deeply divided. Leaves narrow, keeled, unspotted. Inflor
escence densely flowered. Perianth segments more or less clustered; lip three-lobed; spu
thick, down-pointing, much shorter than ovary. Similar to *Gymnadenia* but with sepals and
petals incurved forming a hood. Two species occur in Europe.

**Small White Orchid** *Leucorchis albida* (L.) E. Meyer ex Patze
12-30cm. Tubers divided to base. Leaves three to five, broadly lanceolate; bracts longer than
ovary. Inflorescence dense, many flowered. Flowers very small, 3-5mm in diameter; sepal
and petals incurved; lip three-lobed; spur short, thickened, less than half length of ovary
Flowers greenish- or yellowish-white.
Local over much of Europe including Iceland and the British Isles, eastwards to N. and W
Russia, in pastures, grassy heaths and mountains to 2500 metres. Flowers May to August.

**Frivald's Frog Orchid** *Leucorchis frivaldii* (Hampe ex Griseb.) Schltr.
14-30cm. Tubers divided about half way to base. Leaves three to four, narrowly lanceolate
bracts about length of ovary. Inflorescence dense, many flowered. Flowers about 5mm in
diameter; sepals and petals incurved forming a hood; lip three-lobed; spur small and slender
1½mm long. Flowers white to pale pink.
Mountains of Rumania, Bulgaria, Albania and Yugoslavia, from 1500 to 2500 metres, growing
in seepage areas and damp pasture. Flowers June to August.

# Pink Frog Orchid *Neottianthe*

Perennial. 10-30cm. Tubers two, globular. Leaves, two lower elliptic; one or two small lanceolat
leaves higher on stem; inflorescence lax, from 6-20 flowered. Sepals lanceolate, united with
petals to form narrow hood; lip deeply three-lobed; spur slender and strongly curved. On
species found locally in Europe and eastwards.

**Pink Frog Orchid** *Neottianthe cucullata* (L.) Schltr.
French *Gymnadenia à capuchon*
10-30cm. Leaves, two basal leaves elliptical with bract-like leaves higher on stem; bracts longe
than ovary. Inflorescence lax, more or less one-sided; sepals acuminate, incurving, forming
spiked helmet; lip three-lobed, slightly reflexed; spur slender, curved downwards and forwards
Flowers lilac-pink.
An uncommon and local orchid from north-eastern Germany, Poland and Russia, growing in
damp moss in conifer forests and mountain meadows. Flowers July and August.

# Frog Orchid *Coeloglossum*

Perennial. 10-35cm. Tubers two, deeply palmate; normally only one tuber at time of flowering
Leaves oval to oblong, unspotted; flower spike moderately dense to lax. Sepals and petal
incurved forming a rounded helmet; lip oblong, strap-like with three lobes at apex; spur smal
and rounded; bracts variable in length, sometimes longer than flowers. Column stumpy
rostellum with two lateral lobes. One European species, widespread and locally common.

**Frog Orchid** *Coeloglossum viride* (L.) Hartm.
French *Orchis grenouille* German *Grüne Hohlzunge* Italian *Testicolo di Volpe*
10-35cm. Leaves two to six, broadly lanceolate below, above narrowly lanceolate; bracts longe
than ovary, sometimes longer than flowers. Inflorescence relatively lax, many flowered. Sepal
and petals united into rounded hood; lip strap-like, three-lobed at apex, median lobe muc
shorter than laterals; spur almost globular, about 2mm long. Flowers greenish or yellowish
green, the helmet and lip often edged reddish; sometimes with purplish or reddish wash ove
entire flower.
Most of Europe including Iceland, Faeroe Islands and British Isles, southwards to centra
Spain, southern Bulgaria and eastwards to Crimea and Caucasus. In south only in mountains
Elsewhere in grassland, scrub and woodland margins. Flowers May to August.

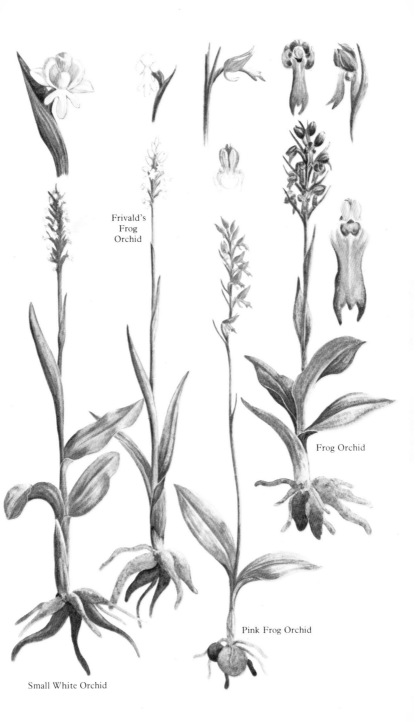

Frivald's
Frog
Orchid

Frog Orchid

Pink Frog Orchid

Small White Orchid

# Butterfly Orchids *Platanthera*

Perennials. 15-60(80)cm. Tubers two, ovoid or fusiform, tapering. Normally two large oval leaves near base of stem; the upper leaves narrow and bract-like. Flower spike lax. Perianth, lateral sepals spreading, dorsal sepal and petals incurved forming a helmet. Lip entire, long and strap-like. Some 80 species are known with centres of abundance in Asia and America.

**Lesser Butterfly Orchid** *Platanthera bifolia* (L.) L. C. M. Richard
French *Orchis à deux feuilles* German *Zweiblättriges Breitkölbchen*
20-50cm. Basal leaves two, elongated oval, with bract-like leaves higher on the stem; bracts about same length as ovary. Inflorescence a lax to fairly dense spike; outer sepals spreading, median sepal and petals incurved forming hood; anther lobes parallel; lip entire, strap-like, pendent; spur 25-30mm much longer than ovary. Flowers white, more or less tinged green or yellowish-green; fragrant.

Almost throughout Europe but less frequent in Mediterranean region; also North Africa; eastwards to Russia and Caucasus. Grows in open woodlands, edges of thickets, heaths and moorland, from sea level to high mountains in various soils. Flowers late May to August.

**Greater Butterfly Orchid** *Platanthera chlorantha* Custer ex Rchb.
French *Orchis verdâtre* German *Grünliches Breitkölbchen*
25-50cm. Basal leaves two, subopposite, elongated oval, higher leaves slender; bracts about length of ovary. Inflorescence lax, many flowered. Flowers average larger and greener than in *P. bifolia* and the anther lobes form an angle with each other, wide apart at the base. Flowers fragrant.

Widespread in Europe including the British Isles, eastwards to Russia, Crimea, Caucasus and Asia Minor. Normally in calcareous soils up to 2000 metres, in woodlands, dry grassland and scrub. Flowers May to August, normally some two weeks ahead of *P. bifolia*.

**Azores Butterfly Orchid** *Platanthera micrantha* (Hochst. ex Seub.) Schltr.
20-50cm. Basal two leaves much larger than others; bracts about same length as ovary. Inflorescence fairly dense, many flowered. Perianth segments rounded at apex; lip oblong, horizontal; spur variable in length, one third to four-fifths length of ovary. Flowers pale green. Endemic to the Azores, growing in mountain grassland and in sphagnum moss amongst *Erica* bushes in acid soil. Flowers June and July.

*Platanthera azorica* Schltr. differs from *P. micrantha* in longer, broader leaves; longer perianth segments and lip; considerably longer spur, 7-8mm, slightly shorter than the ovary. Some doubt its validity as a species.

Azores
Butterfly Orchid

Lesser Butterfly Orchid        Greater Butterfly Orchid

**Algerian Butterfly Orchid** *Platanthera algeriensis* Batt. et Trab.
40-80cm. Closely related to *P. chlorantha*, differing in its more robust habit, longer basal
leaves and relatively longer spur. Anther lobes at an angle to each other but more acute than
in *P. chlorantha*. Flowers yellowish-green.
Algeria and Morocco in mountain woodland at 1400 to 1600 metres. Flowers July and August.

**One-Leaved Butterfly Orchid** *Platanthera obtusata* (Pursh.) L. C. M. Richard
European plants are referable to the ssp. *oligantha* (Turcz.) Hultén, described from eastern
Siberia.
6-20cm. A single elliptical leaf tapering to a sheathing base; bracts about as long as ovary.
Inflorescence lax, three to seven flowered. Lateral sepals horizontal; petals erect, twisted;
lip horizontal or deflexed; spur variable, curved, half as long to as long as ovary. Anther lobe
slightly divergent. Flowers greenish-white.
Arctic Sweden (rare), Finland, Norway and northern Russia; growing in birch and conifer
forest and calcareous mountain heaths. Flowers July to August.

**Northern Butterfly Orchid** *Platanthera hyperborea* (L.) Lindley
6-35cm. Leaves three to five, lanceolate, distributed evenly up stem; bracts longer than ovary.
Inflorescence lax. Lateral sepals spreading; median sepal and petals incurved forming hood;
lip broadly lanceolate, obtuse; spur shorter than ovary. Flowers pale green; fragrant.
An Arctic and subarctic American orchid which also occurs in Iceland. Grows in moist tundra
and moorland. Flowers June and July.

Algerian Butterfly Orchid

One-Leaved Butterfly Orchid

Northern
Butterfly
Orchid

## Green Habenaria *Habenaria*

Perennial. 15-35cm. Tubers two, ovoid, tapering. Two large ovate basal leaves. Flowering spike, 10-30 flowered. Perianth, lateral sepals spreading, dorsal sepal and petals incurved, forming a helmet; lip deeply divided into three strap-like lobes. The single species found in the region covered is endemic to the Canary Islands.

### Three-Lobed Habenaria *Habenaria tridactylites* Lindl.

15-35cm. Basal leaves two, large, ovate; flowering stem leafless; bracts shorter than ovary. Inflorescence lax, 10-30 flowered. Lateral sepals spreading, median sepal and petals incurved to form a helmet; lip deeply three-lobed; spur longer than ovary. Flowers pale green.
Endemic to the Canary Islands, locally common growing on forest cliffs and cliff ledges from 200 to 800 metres. Flowers November to January.

## Two-Leaved Scrub Orchid *Gennaria*

Perennial. 10-30cm. Normally only a single oval tuber at time of flowering. Two heart-shaped leaves alternately on stem; bracts short. Inflorescence moderately dense. Perianth segments slender, incurved forming a tapering hood; lip three-lobed; a very short rounded spur. The single species occurs in the western Mediterranean, Portugal, Madeira and the Canary Islands.

### Two-Leaved Scrub Orchid *Gennaria diphylla* (Link) Parl.

Portuguese *Herva de duas folhos*
10-30cm. Leaves two, heart-shaped, acute, cordate at base; bracts about same length as ovary. Inflorescence in a loose spike, many flowered. Perianth segments convergent forming a tapering hood; lip three-lobed, the median slightly larger than laterals; spur small and rounded. Flowers yellowish-green.
Southern and central Portugal, south-western Spain, Sardinia, North Africa and in Madeira and the Canary Islands. Grows in shady locations, evergreen woods and thickets. Flowers February and March, earlier in the Canary Islands.

## Musk Orchid *Herminium*

Perennial. 7-25cm. Solitary tuber rounded, undivided; young tubers formed at end of underground stolons. Basal leaves two, rarely three, lanceolate or ovoid. Inflorescence rather loose; bracts shorter than ovary. Perianth segments convergent forming a tapering helmet; lip three-lobed; no spur. Flowers sweet scented. One species widely distributed in Europe and eastwards.

### Musk Orchid *Herminium monorchis* (L.) R. Br.

French *Orchis musc* German *Einorche* Dutch *Rechtlip*
7-25cm. Tuber solitary at flowering, others appearing later on slender stolons. Lower leaves two or three, lanceolate; upper leaves bract-like; bracts shorter than ovary. Inflorescence rather lax, many flowered. Sepals and petals form loose tapering helmet; lip three-lobed, the median lobe much longer than laterals; spur barely indicated or absent. Flowers yellowish-green, honey scented.
Over much of Europe east to Russia and Caucasus. Local, absent from extreme north, south-west and most of the Mediterranean area; in grassland and damp meadows up to 2000 metres. In England found only in the south. Flowers June to August.

Musk Orchid flower

Three-Lobed Habenaria

Two-Leaved
Scrub Orchid

Musk Orchid

# Fen Orchid *Liparis*

Perennial. 6-20cm. An ovoid pseudobulb enveloped in dead leaf sheaths; the new pseudobulb at the base of the flowering stem. Two oval basal leaves; flowering stem triangular; raceme loosely two to eight flowered. Perianth segments widely spread with an upward-pointing entire lip; no spur. Column slender. One species in Europe.

**Fen Orchid** *Liparis loeselii* (L.) L. C. M. Richard
French *Liparis de Loesel* German *Zwiebelorchis* Italian *Ofride delleborde*
6-20cm. Stem triangular with two or three basal sheaths enclosing new pseudobulb. Leaves two, subopposite, ovate. Inflorescence lax, three to eight flowered; perianth segments spreading; lip entire, directed upwards; no spur. Flowers yellowish-green.
Local in much of northern, western and central Europe including the British Isles (eastern England and South Wales), eastwards to the Balkans and Russia; absent from the Mediterranean area. Grows in bogs, fens, damp sand-dune slacks and other wet places. Flowers June to August, depending upon latitude and altitude.

# Calypso *Calypso*

Perennial. 10-20cm. Oval or rounded tuber more or less covered with dead sheaths and roots below. A solitary stalked leaf from upper part of tuber. Flowering stem with one or two membranous sheaths; carries a single flower. Perianth segments spreading and ascending; lip slipper-shaped, inflated and narrowed towards apex. Column petaloid, ovate; rostellum small; two distinct viscidia. In Europe found in northern Scandinavia and in northern Russia.

**Calypso** *Calypso bulbosa* (L.) Oakes.
French *Calypso*
10-20cm. Single stalked leaf distinctly veined, elliptic-oblong. Flower arising from axil of linear bract, single. Perianth segments linear-lanceolate, reflexed; lip inflated and slipper-shaped; no spur. Flower, sepals and petals purplish-pink; lip pale pink to whitish with pink and yellow markings.
Northern and central Scandinavia and northern Russia, southwards to 57°N. Grows in marshes and swamps, and wet mossy places in coniferous forests. Flowers May.

# Coralroot *Corallorhiza*

Perennial. 10-30cm. Yellowish-brown or pinkish-white saprophytic species with many branched coral-like rhizomes. Flowering stem with two to four membranous sheaths. Raceme laxly two to ten flowered; bracts small, acuminate. Flower nodding, lateral sepals spreading; dorsal sepal and petals somewhat incurved; lip entire or with tiny lateral lobes at base. Column long; rostellum small; viscidia two. Widespread in Europe and eastwards in alpine and northern habitats.

**Coralroot** *Corallorhiza trifida* Chatel
French *Racine de corail* German *Korallenwurz*
10-30cm. Erect, with two to four sheathing scales along stem; bracts small. Inflorescence lax, two to twelve flowered. Perianth segments more or less spreading; lip obscurely three-lobed; spur absent or barely indicated. Flowers greenish or yellowish-white with reddish-brown spots and margins.
Local in western, northern and central Europe, including British Isles (northern England and Scotland) and Iceland, east to Russia, the Crimea and Caucasus. In south only in mountains. Grows in damp forests, in tundra, damp sand-dune slacks and alpine marshy areas. Flowers May to August.

Coralroot

Fen Orchid

Calypso

## Bog Orchid *Hammarbya*

Perennial. 3-12cm. Pseudobulb enveloped in dead leaf sheaths, new pseudobulb borne abov old one. Two or three oval leaves at base, a swelling in the axil of the upper leaf which develop into following year's tuber. The leaves produce bulbils at their tips which become detached form new plants. Inflorescence lax when in full flower; ovary twisted through 360 degrees s that lip is pointing upwards. Column short; anther persistent. Northern Europe eastward growing in sphagnum moss in bogs.

**Bog Orchid** *Hammarbya paludosa* (L.) O. Kuntze [Syn. *Malaxis paludosa* Rich.]
French *Malaxis des marais* German *Sumpf-weichkraut*
3-12cm. Stem slender, 3-5 angled; leaves two or three, small, oval, usually with terminal bulbils sheathing at base. Inflorescence at first dense, later lax, many flowered. Flowers twiste through 360 degrees so that lip appears uppermost. Sepals spreading, petals reflexed; li entire, smaller than the sepals; no spur. Flowers yellowish-green.
Western, central and northern Europe eastwards to Russia: in Britain most frequent in th north. Grows in acid bogs and marshes amongst sphagnum moss wherein it is extreme difficult to locate. Flowers July to September.

## Single-Leaved Bog Orchid *Malaxis*

Perennial. 10-30cm. Basal pseudobulb enclosed in dry leaf sheaths; a single leaf (rarely tw borne above pseudobulb. Sepals and petals spreading and lip uppermost, flowers twiste through 360 degrees. A rare and apparently decreasing species in Europe, growing in sphagnur

**Single-Leaved Bog Orchid** *Malaxis monophyllos* (L.) Sw. [Syn. *Microstylis monophyll* (L.) Lindl.]
French *Malaxis à une feuille* German *Einblättriges Weichkraut*
10-30cm. Basal pseudobulb surrounded by old leaf sheaths. Leaf solitary, rarely two, man flowered. Sepals, laterals spreading, median pointed downwards; petals slender, widesprea lip pointing upwards; no spur. Flowers green.
Northern, central and eastern Europe to southern Russia. Grows in sphagnum moss in bog wet pastures and woodland; local and very uncommon. Flowers July.

## Creeping Lady's Tresses *Goodyera*

Perennial. 10-50cm. Without tubers but with creeping rhizomes, giving rise to shoots bearin leaf clusters and flowering stems. Leaves four to eight on lower portion of stem, leaves ofte conspicuously reticulated. Inflorescence more or less one-sided; bracts slender, longer tha ovary. Lateral sepals recurved, dorsal sepal united with petals to form a hood; lip slight shorter than sepals, basal part strongly concave, distal part flat; no spur. Two species, on widespread, one endemic to Madeira.

**Creeping Lady's Tresses** *Goodyera repens* (L.) R. Br.
French *Goodyère rampante* German *Moosorchis* Italian *Satirio serpeggiante*
10-25cm. Basal leaves three to six, oval; upper leaves reduced to sheaths; bracts longer tha ovary. Inflorescence slender, lax, often with slight spiral twist. Lateral sepals spreadin median sepal and petals forming a tight hood; lip strongly concave at base; no spur. Flowe white, fragrant.
Western, northern and central Europe eastwards to Russia, the Crimea and Caucasus. Foun from sea level to over 2000 metres, growing in coniferous and mixed woodland. Flowers Jul and August.

**Madeiran Lady's Tresses** *Goodyera macrophylla* Lowe
20-50cm. Basal leaves five to seven, broadly lanceolate; upper leaves reduced to sheath bracts as long as ovary. Inflorescence relatively dense, many flowered. Sepals and petals mor or less incurved forming a hood; lip shorter than sepals; no spur. Flowers white.
Endemic to Madeira, in damp woodlands. Flowers April to September.

Bog Orchid

Madeiran
Lady's Tresses

Creeping Lady's Tresses

Single-Leaved Bog Orchid

# Lady's Tresses *Spiranthes*

Perennials. 8-25(30)cm. Roots clustered, more or less tuberous. Leaves variable; flowers arranged spirally around stem. Sepals united forming a tube-like hood; lip entire, wavy at edges and apex; no spur. Rostellum has narrow lobes with single viscidium between; anther largely concealed by rostellum. A group of approximately thirty species, four occurring in the region covered.

### Autumn Lady's Tresses *Spiranthes spiralis* (L.) Chevall
[Syn. *Spiranthes autumnalis* L. C. M. Richard]
French *Spiranthe d'automne* German *Herbst-Wendelähre*
6-20cm. Leaves oval, bluish-green, in rosette which withers before flowers open; following year's rosette appears alongside stem during flowering. Stem with small bract-like sheaths; bracts longer than ovary. Inflorescence slender with 6-20 flowers in spiral. Outer sepals somewhat reflexed; median sepal and petals forming a hood which together with the lip forms a tube-like structure; lip with wavy apex; no spur. Flowers greenish-white, scented.
Western, central and southern Europe, northwards to eastern Denmark; common in southern half of England and Wales. Mainly a lowland species but occurs up to 1000 metres. In pastures, especially in short turf, in a variety of soils. Flowers August and September.

### Pink Lady's Tresses *Spiranthes sinensis* (Pers.) Ames.
[Syn. *Spiranthes amoena* (Bieb.) Sprengel]
15-30cm. Basal leaves four to five, erect, linear-lanceolate; upper leaves bract-like; bracts longer than ovary. Inflorescence dense, many flowered. Sepals, petals and lip form a tube-like flower; lip with two callosities near base; no spur. Flowers white to pale rose, rarely pink.
Recorded from the Volga-Kama region of Russia. Grows in wet meadows near rivers and lakes and in peat bogs. Flowers July and August.

### Summer Lady's Tresses *Spiranthes aestivalis* (Poiret) L. C. M. Richard
French *Spiranthe d'été* German *Sommer Wendelähre* Italian *Viticcini d'aestate*
12-30cm. Basal leaves four to six, linear-lanceolate, suberect; scale-like leaves above; bracts slightly longer than ovary. Inflorescence lax, spiral. Perianth segments forming tube-like structure; lip longer than sepals, with margins curled upwards and apex crenulate; no spur. Flowers yellowish-white to white, scented.
Widespread but local in western, southern and central Europe, eastwards to Turkey and Russia; also North Africa. In damp grassland and mountain pasture up to 1200 metres. Flowers June to August.

### Irish Lady's Tresses *Spiranthes romanzoffiana* Cham.
French *Spiranthe dressé*
12-25cm. Leaves five to eight, linear-lanceolate; bracts longer than ovary. Inflorescence dense, many flowered in three spiral rows. Sepals and lip forming tube-like structure; lip sharply deflexed towards apex; no spur. Flowers creamy-white to greenish-white.
In Europe confined to localities in Ireland, western Scotland and south-western England; in acid bogs and peat marshes. Flowers late July and August. Main distribution, North America.

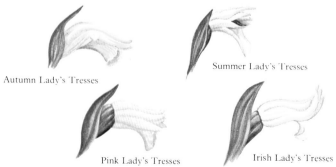

Autumn Lady's Tresses

Summer Lady's Tresses

Pink Lady's Tresses

Irish Lady's Tresses

Pink Lady's Tresses

Autumn Lady's Tresses

Summer Lady's Tresses

Irish Lady's Tresses

## Bird's Nest Orchid *Neottia*

Perennial, but sometimes monocarpic, dying after flowering. 20-50cm. Roots forming a dense mass slightly resembling a bird's nest. Saprophytic, no leaves; the stem with brown sheathing scales; flowers in lax or fairly dense raceme; bracts lanceolate, longer or shorter than ovary. Perianth segments incurved forming a loose hood; lip divided at apex; no spur. Column elongated with rather long beak; anther projecting over beak. This orchid has been recorded as flowering underground on rare occasions. Widespread in Europe and eastwards.

**Bird's Nest Orchid** *Neottia nidus-avis* (L.) L. C. M. Richard
French *Néottie nid d'oiseau* German *Nestwurz* Italian *Nido d'uccello*
20-40cm. Saprophytic, entire plant yellowish-brown without leaves; flowering stem with bract-like brown scales; bracts shorter than ovary. Inflorescence dense. Sepals incurved forming a hood; lip deeply two-lobed at apex; no spur. Flowers yellowish-brown, honey-scented.
Throughout Europe east to Russia, Crimea and Caucasus; North Africa. Grows in humid leaf-mould in woodlands, often in deep shade. Flowers May to July.

## Twayblades *Listera*

Perennials. 5-60cm. Plants with slender roots without tubers. A pair of opposite broad leaves on stem. Perianth segments incurved forming a loose hood; lip strap-like, divided at apex; no spur. Column short; beak straight, anther overlying beak. Approximately ten species occur in the cold and temperate areas of Asia and North America, two of which are found in Europe.

**Common Twayblade** *Listera ovata* (L.) R. Br.
French *Grande Listère* German *Wiesen-Zweiblatt* Italian *Orchide-di-primavera*
30-60cm. Leaves two, broad oval, subopposite, placed low down on stem; bracts very short. Inflorescence a fairly lax spike, many flowered. Sepals incurved forming a loose hood; lip strap-like, hanging vertical, deeply divided at apex; no spur. Flowers green or yellowish-green sometimes tinged reddish-brown.
Over most of Europe to 70°N; eastwards to Russia; less common in Mediterranean region from sea level to 1800 metres. Grows in coniferous and other woodlands, scrub and grassland in shade or exposed to sun. Flowers May to June.

**Lesser Twayblade** *Listera cordata* (L.) R. Br.
French *Listère en coeur* German *Moor-Zweiblatt*
5-20cm. Leaves two, heart-shaped, sub-opposite, midway up stem; bracts very short. Inflorescence lax, few flowered. Sepals less incurved than in *L. ovata*, forming a loose hood; lip strap-like, three-lobed, the laterals very small; median lobe forked for half its length; no spur. Flowers reddish-green to reddish-brown.
Widespread in Europe, eastwards to Russia and the Caucasus, from sea-level in the north to mountains further south, up to 2000 metres. Grows in coniferous woodlands, moorland amongst heather and in peat bogs; flowers June to early September.

Bird's Nest Orchid

Lesser
Twayblade

Common Twayblade

## Spurred Coralroot *Epipogium*

Perennial. 5-20cm. Saprophytic. Rhizome branched, resembling coral, with hair-like rootlet and horizontal filiform stolons. Stem swollen at base. No leaves, only a few sheathing scales Inflorescence loosely one to five flowered. Perianth segments, sepals linear, petals lanceolate lip directed upwards, divided into three lobes, laterals short and rounded, median lobe ovat to triangular; spur 8mm, rounded at apex. Column short, rostellum small. A rare specie growing in decaying leaf debris.

### Spurred Coralroot *Epipogium aphyllum* (F. W. Schmidt) Sw.
French *Epipogon sans feuilles* German *Ohnblatt*

5-20cm. Saprophytic; no leaves. Stem swollen at base with two to five short brownish sheathing scales; bracts small. Inflorescence lax, one to five flowered; flowers pendent on short slende stalks. Perianth segments curved downwards; lip three-lobed, the laterals short and rounded the median lobe triangular to ovate pointing upwards; spur thick and slightly curved, rounded at apex. Flowers yellowish- or reddish-white with violet markings; lip white or pinkish with violet spots and papillae; spur yellowish or pinkish-white.

Over most of Europe to 66°N in Scandinavia, southwards to the Pyrenees, the central Apennines north-western Greece, Russia, Crimea and Caucasus. Very rare in England, in some southern counties. Grows in woods and forests amongst decaying vegetable matter. Flowers July and August. Everywhere local and very uncommon.

## Violet Limodore *Limodorum*

Perennial. 40-80cm. Saprophytic. Root system a rhizome from which spring thick tuber-like roots. No leaves; stem robust with numerous sheathing scales. Inflorescence lax, between ₄ and 20 flowered . Perianth segments spreading; lip triangular; spur long and slender. Column long, a single viscidium. Represented by a single species.

### Violet Limodore *Limodorum abortivum* (L.) Swartz
French *Limodore à feuilles avortées* German *Dingel* Italian *Fiammone* or *Fior-di-legno*

40-80cm. Leafless saprophytic. Stem robust with many sheathing scales; stem and scales brownish, mauve or violet. Inflorescence lax, 4-20 flowered. Perianth segments spreading; lip entire, triangular with wavy margin; slender curved spur nearly as long as ovary. Flowers violet, the lip violet and yellow. Var. *rubrum* from southern Turkey has rose-pink not violet flowers. Local in central and southern Europe, extending north-westwards to Belgium, eastwards to Caucasus; North Africa. Grows in calcareous soils from sea-level to 1500 metres in mixed and coniferous woodlands, shady banks, bushy grasslands. Flowers April to July.

Violet Limodore

Spurred Coralroot

# White Helleborines *Cephalanthera*

Perennials. 20-60cm. Root system a creeping rhizome with roots. No tubers. Leaves spaced evenly along stem. Flowers stalkless, erect on spirally twisted, stalk-like ovaries. Perianth segments convergent, flowers not opening widely; lip constricted in middle dividing the concave basal section, the hypochile, and the distal part, the epichile, which normally has a recurved apex and longitudinal ridges. Column erect, lengthened. Spur very short or absent. The closely related genus *Epipactis* has flowers distinctly stalked and held horizontally or drooping. Five species occur in Europe.

### Large White Helleborine *Cephalanthera damasonium* (Miller) Druce
French *Céphalanthère blanche* German *Weisses Waldvögelein* Italian *Elleborine giallognola*
15-60cm. Stem leafy, leaves from oblong-ovate at base to lanceolate; bracts broad, longer than ovary. Inflorescence lax, three to twelve flowered. Perianth segments convergent and flower not opening fully; lip shorter than sepals with 3 to 5 orange-yellow ridges on epichile; no spur. Flowers white, creamy within with an orange-yellow mark at base of hypochile.
Widespread over western, central and southern Europe, northwards to England and south-western Russia, Crimea and Caucasus; North Africa. Grows in shady woodlands especially of beech, in thickets and plantations. Flowers May to July.

*Cephalanthera damasonium* (Miller) Druce ssp. *caucasica* (Kränzl.)?, known only from Talysh in the Caucasus, has shorter bracts, half the length of ovary, and only three ridges on epichile.

### Sword-Leaved Helleborine *Cephalanthera longifolia* (Hudson) Fritsch
French *Céphalanthère à longues feuilles* Italian *Elleborine bianca* German *Langblättriges Waldvögelein*
15-60cm. Leaves numerous, lanceolate to linear, erect; bracts shorter than ovary. Inflorescence moderately dense to lax, 10-20 flowered. Perianth segments not opening fully but more widely than White Helleborine; lip heart-shaped with small orange patch at base of hypochile, 5-7 ridges on epichile; no spur.
Widespread over most of Europe except the extreme north and much of the north-east; also occurs North Africa, Crimea, Caucasus, Turkey and Iran. Grows in woodlands and plantations. Flowers April to early July.

Large White
Helleborine

Sword-Leaved
Helleborine

**Red Helleborine** *Cephalanthera rubra* (L.) L. C. M. Richard
French *Céphalanthère rouge* German *Rotes Waldvögelein* Italian
*Elleborine rosea*
20-60cm. Stem slender; leaves five to eight, lanceolate to
linear-lanceolate; bracts as long as the flowers. Inflorescence
lax, three to ten flowered, flowers opening more fully than
related species; sepals spreading; lip, epichile pointed with
reddish margin and 7-9 narrow yellow ridges; spur barely
indicated or absent. Flowers bright pink, sometimes tinged lilac.
Most of Europe northwards to southern England and southern
Finland, eastwards to Russia, Crimea and Caucasus; also in
North Africa. Grows in wooded areas and thickets from sea-level
to 1800 metres, on limestone soils. Flowers May to early August.

**Hooded Helleborine** *Cephalanthera cucullata* Boiss. & Heldr.
15-30cm. Stem with sheathing leaves; bracts longer than
flowers. Inflorescence relatively lax, 7-24 flowered; perianth
segments opening partially; lip, hypochile with rounded lateral
lobes, epichile heart-shaped with 3-6 ridges; spur conical,
1-2mm long. Flowers white or pale pink. Short spur and
sheathing leaves distinguish this species from close allies.
Endemic to Crete, growing in mountain forest and in thickets.
Flowers end of March to early June.

**Eastern Hooded Helleborine** *Cephalanthera epipactoides*
Fisch. & E. Mayer
30-100cm. A more robust plant with a longer spur than
*C. cucullata*. Lower leaves sheathing the stem, upper leaves
horizontal, broadly lanceolate, acute; bracts as long or longer
than ovary. Inflorescence more or less dense, 10-40 flowered;
perianth segments not opening fully; lip, hypochile with
truncate lateral lobes, epichile triangular with 7-9 ridges; spur
3-5mm long, subacute. Flowers white.
The northern Aegean Islands and Turkey (western Anatolia),
in coniferous woodlands and scrub on limestone. Flowers late
March to early June.

*Cephalanthera epipactoides* ssp. *kurdica* (Bornm. ap Kränzl.)
Sunderm.
25-65cm. Similar to nominate race but flowers red or deep pink,
inflorescence usually more lax.
Occurs in eastern Turkey, northern Syria and Iran.

*Cephalanthera epipactoides* ssp. *floribunda* (Woronow) Sunderm.
Similar to *C.e. kurdica* but ovary and lip hairy; flowers reputed
to be yellowish-white.
Known from eastern Pontus, Turkey and the Caucasus.

Hooded Helleborine

...ed Helleborine

Eastern Hooded Helleborine

Eastern Hooded Helleborine
ssp. *kurdica*

# Helleborines *Epipactis*

Perennials. 20-80(100)cm. Plants have rhizomes and fleshy roots but no tubers. Stem with evenly spaced leaves. Flowers on distinctly twisted stalks, drooping or horizontal; ovary not spirally twisted. Perianth segments either spreading, or incurved forming a lax helmet; lip composed of two sections, often jointed in centre, the basal part, the hypochile, forming a cup, the apical part, the epichile, enlarged into a heart-shaped, triangular or rounded down-pointing lobe; no spur. Column short; rostellum large and spherical but absent in some species. The genus *Cephalanthera* has erect, stalkless flowers and a spirally twisted ovary.

**Marsh Helleborine** *Epipactis palustris* (L.) Crantz.
French *Epipactis marais* German *Echte Sumpfwurz* Italian *Mughetti pendolini*
15-50cm. Leaves four to eight, oblong-lanceolate, upper leaves smaller; bracts, the lower ones longer than the ovary, the upper shorter. Inflorescence lax, 7-14 flowered; flowers open fully, perianth segments spreading; lip, hypochile slightly concave with erect triangular lobes on each side; epichile connected by narrow joint, margin undulate; no spur. Rostellum present. Flowers, sepals greenish-grey outside, reddish inside; petals whitish with red-brown stripes; lip whitish with reddish veins.
Most of Europe except the extreme north and parts of the Mediterranean region, eastwards to northern Turkey, Russia, Crimea, Caucasus and Iran. In marshes, damp sand-dune slacks and wet moorlands, generally in colonies, from sea-level to 1600 metres. Flowers June to August.

**Scarce Marsh Helleborine** *Epipactis veratrifolia* Boiss.
[Syn. *E. consimilis* D. Don]
50-100cm. Leaves eight to twelve, broad to slender lanceolate; bracts very long, lower ones twice length of flowers. Inflorescence lax, 15-30 flowered, flowers horizontal to slightly drooping; perianth segments spreading, flowers opening fully; lip, hypochile slender, up-curved with rounded basal lobes, epichile triangular, attached to hypochile by narrow connective joint; no spur. Flowers deep wine-red and greenish-white; epichile white crossed by red band.
A rare and very local orchid recorded from Cyprus, eastern Turkey, Lebanon, the Caucasus and Iran. Grows in hillside seepages and moist mountain meadows, from 500 to 2000 metres. Flowers June to August.

Scarce Marsh
Helleborine

Marsh Helleborine

**Broad-Leaved Helleborine** *Epipactis helleborine* (L.) Crantz.
French *Epipactis à larges feuilles* German *Brietblättrige Sumpfwurz* Italian *Elleborine crestata* 35-80cm. Leaves four to ten, in spiral, broadly oval, often tinged purplish; bracts at base longer than flowers, shorter above. Inflorescence dense, many flowered, normally forming a one-sided flowering spike; flowers opening fully, horizontal to slightly drooping. Perianth segments spreading, sepals and petals broad, greenish; petals pinkish-violet at base; lip, hypochile cupshaped, greenish outside, dark reddish-brown inside; epichile ovate with apex recurved, greenish-white, pink or purplish; two basal protuberances; rostellum persistent.
Throughout most of Europe from sea-level to 2000 metres, east to Russia, Crimea, Caucasus; also North Africa. Grows in shady places in both coniferous and mixed woodlands, sand-dune slacks, thickets and scrub. Flowers June to September, depending upon latitude and altitude.

**Cyprus Helleborine** *Epipactis troodii* H. Lindb. 15-45cm Leaves three to five, in spiral, broadly lanceolate, often tinged purplish on underside; bracts broad, longer than ovary. Inflorescence lax, 5 to 10 flowered; flowers horizontal. Perianth segments spreading, sepals broad, green; petals pale olive green; lip, epichile triangular, reddish.
Endemic to Cyprus, growing in coniferous forests on Mt Troodos between 1200 and 2000 metres. Flowers June and July.

Cyprus
Helleborine

Broad-Leaved Helleborine

**Violet Helleborine** *Epipactis purpurata* Sm.
French *Epipactis pourpre* German *Violettrote Sumpfwurz*
20-70cm. Usually growing in clumps. Leaves six to ten, in spiral, greyish-green tinged purple; bracts longer than flowers. Inflorescence dense, many flowered; flowers horizontal to semi-pendent when mature. Perianth segments spreading, sepals and petals broad, the former green outside, whitish inside; petals pinkish-white; lip, hypochile cup-shaped, greenish outside, mottled violet inside; epichile triangular, acute, with recurved apex; two or three basal protuberances, whitish; rostellum present.
Northern, western and central Europe, extending south-eastwards to Bulgaria; southern England. In open woodlands on calcareous soils. Flowers August, later than Broad-leaved Helleborine.

**Eastern Violet Helleborine** *Epipactis condensata* Boiss. ex D. P. Young
30-75cm. Often growing in clumps. Leaves acute oval to lanceolate, in spiral; leaves and stem tinged purplish-red; bracts slightly longer than flowers; flowers horizontal. Perianth segments broad, spreading, green; lip, hypochile cup-shaped, dark purplish-red; epichile heart-shaped, greenish, with two-marked reddish basal protuberances; rostellum present.
Coniferous mountain forests in Cyprus, Turkey and Lebanon. Flowers June to early August.

**Mueller's Helleborine** *Epipactis muelleri* Godfery
25-70cm. Leaves seven to ten, in spiral, broadly lanceolate, acute; bracts longer than flowers, upper ones shorter. Inflorescence lax, 4-20 flowered, in a one-sided spike. Perianth segments moderately incurved, green or whitish; lip, hypochile cup-shaped, inside reddish; epichile heart-shaped, broader than long, whitish; rostellum absent.
South-eastern France, western Germany, Belgium, Holland, Luxembourg and Vaud in Switzerland. Local and uncommon. In open woodlands and mixed grass and scrub. Flowers from July to August.

Eastern Violet
Helleborine

Violet Helleborine

Mueller's Helleborine

**Pendulous-Flowered Helleborine** *Epipactis phyllanthes* G. E. Smith
20-45cm. Leaves three to six, broad oval, arranged in two rows, not spiral; bracts longer than flowers, upper bracts shorter. Inflorescence lax, 12-30 flowered; flowers pendulous, usually not opening fully. Sepals and petals pale yellowish-green, the petals sometimes tinged violet; lip, hypochile shallowly hollowed; epichile oval, usually longer than wide, greenish-white to pinkish-white; rostellum absent. A variable species, particularly as regard lip structure, and several species have been named on minor and variant characters. These include *Epipactis confusa* D. P. Young from southern Sweden, Denmark and northern Germany. This is a less robust plant than *E. phyllanthes* with leaves narrower and flowers which open a little more fully; the lip is pinker. The consensus of opinion, however, is that this cannot be recognized in a higher category than a variety. Northern, western and west-central Europe including Britain. Grows in damp areas especially coastal sand-dune slacks, open woodlands and conifer plantations; flowers June to early September.

**Pontus Helleborine** *Epipactis pontica* Taubenh.
15-30cm. Leaves three to five, narrowly lanceolate, in two rows on stem; bracts slightly longer than flowers, upper bracts shorter. Inflorescence lax, 7-15 flowered, flowers pendulous, not opening fully. Sepals and petals incurved, green; lip, epichile rounded at apex, not pointed, white with green patch at base.
Known only from north-eastern Turkey in central and eastern Pontus, from 500 to 1500 metres. Grows on limestone in beech woods near the coast of the Black Sea. Flowers August and September.

Pontus
Helleborine

Pendulous-Flowered
Helleborine

var. *confusa*

**Persian Helleborine** *Epipactis persica* Hauskn. ap Soó
10-50cm. Leaves three to four, broadly lanceolate to oval, in two rows up stem; bracts longer than flowers, upper bracts shorter. Inflorescence lax, 5-12 flowered; flowers horizontal, slightly pendulous when mature. Sepals and petals broad, spreading, pale green to whitish; lip, epichile triangular, greenish white. Flowers opening fully.
A local and uncommon species known from Turkey, Iran and Afghanistan. Grows in both coniferous and mixed woodlands from 800 to 2500 metres. Flowers June and July.

**Narrow-Lipped Helleborine** *Epipactis leptochila* (Godfery) Godfery
30-60cm. Leaves five to ten, yellowish-green to dark green, oval to lanceolate, in two rows up stem; bracts large and longer than flowers, upper bracts slender and shorter. Inflorescence lax, 7-20 flowered; flowers horizontal to pendulous when mature; sometimes not opening fully. Sepals and petals more or less spreading, yellowish-green; lip, hypochile reddish; epichile long and pointed, yellowish-green margined white; rostellum usually absent.
Northern, western and central Europe including British Isles; on calcareous soils in shady woodlands, especially beech, amongst willow scrub in sand-dune slacks and in shady thickets. Flowers July and early August.

**Dune Helleborine** *Epipactis dunensis* (T. et T. A. Steph.) Godfery
20-40cm. Leaves seven to ten, broadly lanceolate, yellowish-green, in two rows; bracts longer than flowers, upper bracts shorter. Inflorescence lax, 7-20 flowered; flowers more or less horizontal, usually not opening fully. Sepals and petals pale green; lip, hypochile mottled red inside, epichile triangular, greenish-white with tip often recurved; no rostellum.
Northern England and North Wales, growing in sand-dune slacks and coastal conifer plantations; flowers June and July. Records of this species from continental Europe probably refer to *Epipactis muelleri*.

Persian
Helleborine

Narrow-Lipped Helleborine

Dune Helleborine

**Dark Red Helleborine** *Epipactis atrorubens* (Hoffm.) Schultes
French *Epipactis rouge* German *Dunkelrote Sumpfwurz*
20-60cm. Leaves five to ten, oval to broadly lanceolate, purplish on underside, arranged in two rows on stem; lower bracts as long as flowers, upper bracts shorter. Inflorescence fairly lax, many flowered; flowers horizontal to drooping, opening fully. Sepals, petals and lip deep purple to magenta or brick-red; lip, epichile wider than long with a recurved tip and protuberances at base; rostellum present; flowers fragrant.
Throughout most of Europe including British Isles, eastwards to Russia, Crimea, Caucasus and Iran. Rare in Mediterranean area. Occurs from sea-level to 2200 metres. Grows in rocky limestone areas, woodland margins, amongst bushes and grass and in sand-dune slacks. Flowers May to August, depending upon altitude. Var. *borbasii* Soó from Hungary has very broad, short leaves.

*Epipactis atrorubens* ssp. *parviflora* A. et C. Nieschalk has rounder leaves and very small pale brown or greenish flowers.
From mountains in southern Spain.

**Small-Leaved Helleborine** *Epipactis microphylla* (Ehrh.) Swartz
French *Epipactis à petites feuilles* German *Kleinblättrige Sumpfwurz*
15-45cm. Leaves three to six, oval to lanceolate, very small, arranged in a spiral; bracts longer than ovary, upper bracts shorter. Inflorescence lax, 4-15 flowered; flowers horizontal to slightly pendulous, opening fully. Sepals and petals reddish-green outside, greenish-white inside; lip, epichile whitish to pale pink; rostellum present.
Southern and central Europe, eastwards to Turkey, Russia, Crimea and Caucasus; found both at low altitudes and in mountains up to 1200 metres. Grows in beech and other woodlands on limestone. Flowers May to August.

Dark Red Helleborine

Small-Leaved Helleborine

# GLOSSARY OF BOTANICAL TERMS

*Numerals in Glossary refer to line drawings in margins.*

**Acid soils:** those with few basic alkaline minerals, e.g. peaty soils.

**Acuminate:** becoming gradually narrower towards the tip.

**Acute:** with a tip that narrows abruptly to a sharp point.

**Albino:** a plant in which the flowers are lacking the usual colour pigments.

**Alternate:** term applied to leaves that are attached at different levels along a stem; not opposite.

**Anther:** that part of a stamen containing the pollen; it is usually divided longitudinally into two parts joined by a connective tissue (1).

**Apex, apical:** the tip or topmost point of a structure.

**Appendage:** a part attached to another larger structure.

**Attenuate:** tapering gradually.

**Axil:** the angle (upper) where a leaf joins the stem.

**Bi-:** a prefix, meaning two or twice.

**Bifid, bilobed:** cleft in two no further than to the middle.

**Bifurcate:** forked, with two equal branches.

**Bog:** swampy habitat on wet, acid, peaty soil.

**Bract:** small leaf-like or scale-like structure from axil of which a flower stalk often arises.

**Bulbils:** tiny bulb-like organs growing at tips of leaves which break off to form new plants (2).

**Bursicle:** a pouch-like flap covering the sticky disc (the viscidium) preventing it from drying. This is pushed back by an insect visiting the flower (3).

**Calcareous soils:** soils containing lime; chalky.

**Campanulate:** bell-shaped.

**Capsule:** a dry fruit formed from two or more fused carpels which splits open when ripe to release the seeds (4).

**Carpel:** one of the sections of the female part of the flower, in orchids fused together into the fruit.

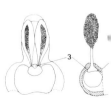

**Caudicle:** the lower stalk-like part of the pollinium, connecting the pollen masses to the viscidium (5).

**Chlorophyll:** the green colouring matter in plants.

**Ciliate:** fringed with hair along the margin.

**Cleistogamous:** self-fertilized in the unopened flower.

**Column:** the structure in the centre of an orchid

flower formed by the fusion of stigma and stamens.
Variable in shape in different orchids (6).

**Connective:** tissue connecting two anthers (7).

**Converging:** two or more organs separated at the
base with tips coming together.

**Cordate:** heart-shaped.

**Corm:** the enlarged fleshy base of a stem, bulb-like
but of different structure and solid.

**Deciduous:** not bearing green leaves throughout the
year.

**Deflexed:** bent downwards.

**Dehiscent:** splitting open, as in dry orchid capsules,
to allow the seeds to escape.

**Dentate:** toothed.

**Downy:** with a covering of soft hairs.

**Dunes:** a habitat of wind-blown sand, usually
lime-rich, with damp hollows called slacks
supporting vegetation.

**Ecology:** the study of plants and animals in relation to
their environment.

**Elliptic:** oval, narrowing to a rounded end.

**Endemic:** native of and confined to a given area or
region.

**Entire:** whole, without teeth, lobes or indentations.

**Epichile:** the outer section of the lip in those species
where the lip is divided into two distinct parts by
constriction of the middle, as in the genera
*Epipactis* and *Cephalanthera* (8).

**Fen:** wet habitat on calcareous soils, not acid as is a bog.

**Fertile:** capable of bearing viable fruit.

**Filament:** the thread-like stalk of the stamen bearing
the anthers.

**Filiform:** thread-like or very slender.

**Foliaceous:** resembling a leaf in texture and
appearance.

**Form:** a slight variant of a species, usually occurring
sporadically.

**Free:** not joined together.

**Galea:** a helmet or hood-shaped formation.

**Genus (plural genera):** the term used in
classification for a group of closely related species.
A number of genera form a family. The generic
name is the first part of a plant's scientific name
e.g. *Orchis* (genus) *patens* (species).

**Glabrous:** smooth, without hairs.
**Globose:** globular, globe-shaped, spherical.

**Habit:** general appearance of a plant.
**Habitat:** the conditions of environment in which a plant grows; factors involved include climate, soil, supply of water, altitude, associated plants etc.
**Heath:** habitat on acid soils with characteristic plants such as heaths and heathers.
**Herbs:** fleshy, non-woody plants.
**Hispid:** with coarse, stiff hairs.
**Humus:** decomposing organic matter in the soil.
**Hyaline:** thin and translucent.
**Hybrid:** a plant resulting from cross-breeding between two different species, and showing some characters of each parent. Often but not always infertile.
**Hybrid-swarm:** large numbers of hybrid plants growing together, showing varying characters of the two parent species.
**Hymenoptera:** insects belonging to the family Hymenoptera, including wasps, bees, ants, saw-flies and ichneumons, some of which are involved in the fertilization of certain orchids.
**Hypochile:** the basal section of the lip where the lip is divided into two distinct parts, as in the genera *Epipactis* and *Cephalanthera* (9).

**Inferior:** below; orchids have an inferior ovary i.e. one situated below the flower.
**Inflated:** blown-up, bladdery.
**Inflorescence:** the flowering section of a plant.
**Internode:** that part of the stem between two nodes; the section of stem between leaves.
**Irregular flower:** not symmetrical; all orchids are irregular flowers.

**Keeled:** with a raised ridge.

**Labellum:** another name for the lip. The modified median petal in an orchid flower, usually differing markedly in size, colour and form from the other two petals (10), (12d).
**Lanceolate:** spear or lance-shaped; tapering towards apex; several times longer than wide.
**Lateral:** borne on each side.
**Lax:** loose and spreading as opposed to densely packed or dense.

**Lime:** limestone rock; soils formed on limestone or chalk, the opposite of acid soils.

**Linear:** long and narrow, nearly parallel-sided (e.g. of a leaf).

**Lingulate:** tongue-shaped.

**Lip:** *see* **Labellum.**

**Littoral:** on sea shore or near the sea.

**Lobe:** any segment or division of an organ e.g. a three-lobed lip is a lip divided into three segments.

**Lobule:** subdivision of a lobe.

**Maculate:** spotted.

**Marsh:** water-logged ground but not on peat.

**Maquis:** thicket of shrubs and scattered trees, typical of the Mediterranean region.

**Membranous:** thin, dry, parchment or paper-like.

**Midrib:** central vein of leaf, often raised.

**Monocarpic:** flowering once and then dying.

**Monotypic:** having only one exponent e.g. a genus with but one species.

**Montane:** pertaining to mountains.

**Morphology:** the study of the structure, form and appearance of plants.

**Mycorrhiza:** the association of a fungus with the roots or other parts of a plant.

**Mycorrhizome:** the initial plant-body produced following the germination of an orchid seed; it is always infected with an appropriate fungus.

**Nectar:** sweet substance produced by many plants and attractive to insects.

**Net-veined:** a leaf in which the veins are not all parallel.

**Neutral soils:** soils in which acid and alkaline constituents are balanced.

**Node:** point of origin of leaves on a stem.

**Oblong:** elongated but relatively wide; nearly parallel-sided (e.g. of a leaf).

**Obovate:** as **Ovate** but with the broadest part towards the apex.

**Obtuse:** blunt or rounded at end.

**Opposite:** leaves growing opposite to each other along a stem; in pairs.

**Oval:** broadly elliptic.

**Ovary:** the base of the reproductive organ (pistil) containing the embryonic seeds. The ovary is always situated below the rest of the flower in orchids (11).

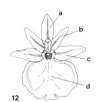

**Ovate:** shaped like the outline of an egg, the broadest part towards the base.

**Papillose:** having small protuberances.

**Palmate:** divided with finger-like lobes e.g. some orchid tubers.

**Pedicel:** the stalk of a single flower.

**Pellucid:** clear, almost transparent.

**Pendulous:** drooping or hanging.

**Perennial:** a plant which survives for more than two years, usually flowering each year.

**Perianth:** the outer, non-reproductive parts of an orchid flower (12), comprising three outer segments called sepals (a & c), and three inner segments, the petals (b & d).

**Petaloid:** petal-like.

**Petals:** the three inner parts of the perianth in an orchid flower; the two simple petals on each side, and the median petal usually modified and termed the lip or labellum.

**Pistil:** the female reproductive organ, comprising style, stigma and ovary.

**Pollen:** small grains which contain the male reproductive cells.

**Pollinium (plural pollinia):** a mass of pollen grains held together by threads or adhesives (13).

**Polymorphic:** variable, having more than one form.

**Pseudobulb:** swelling at base of stem resembling a bulb; usually serves as a water storage organ. Found only in the genera *Liparis*, *Hammarbya* and *Malaxis* in European orchids (14).

**Pubescent:** with soft downy hairs.

**Pyramidal:** pyramid-shaped.

**Pyriform:** pear-shaped.

**Raceme:** an elongated inflorescence arranged singly along a stem, each flower on its own stalk; youngest flowers at the apex.

**Racemose:** having flowers in a raceme-type inflorescence.

**Recurved:** bent backwards or downwards in a curve.

**Reflexed:** bent abruptly backwards or downwards.

**Reticulated:** net-veined, with the lateral veins connected by small veins like the meshes of a net.

**Rhizome:** a root-like stem growing below the ground with roots growing downwards and leaves and shoots upwards.

**Ribbed:** with the leaf veins prominent.

**Rosette:** leaf arrangement at ground level radiating from base of stem.

**Rostellum:** a small beak; the slender extension from the upper edge of the stigma; the sterile third stigma of an orchid flower (15).

**Saprophyte, saprophytic:** a plant which derives its nourishment from dead organic matter. Such plants do not possess chlorophyll.

**Scale:** a thin, dry flap of tissue, usually a modified leaf.

**Sepals:** the three outer sections of the orchid flower— the upper or dorsal sepal and one on each side, the lateral sepals.

**Sessile:** without a stalk.

**Sheaths:** the base of a leaf which envelops the stem; the lower leaves usually consist entirely of sheath, the leaf-blade not being developed.

**Sinuate:** with the outline of the margin strongly wavy.

**Spatulate:** spoon-shaped.

**Species:** a unit of classification indicating populations of similar plants which interbreed and produce fertile progeny. Related species are classified under the heading of genus.

**Speculum:** an often strikingly coloured patch in the centre of the labellum, esp. in *Ophrys* (16).

**Spike:** elongated flower cluster; flowers stalkless or nearly so.

**Spur:** a hollow, tubular extension on a flower; often containing nectar (17).

**Stamen:** one of the pollen-bearing male reproductive organs of a flower.

**Staminode:** an infertile or rudimentary stamen without pollen.

**Stigma:** that part of the female organ which receives the male pollen (18).

**Stolon:** horizontal stem spreading below ground, which roots at tip to give rise to a new plant.

**Subspecies:** the unit of classification below species; often used to denote morphologically distinct geographical populations which are capable of interbreeding freely if brought together and are therefore included in the same species.

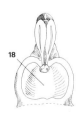

**Succulent:** fleshy, juicy and usually thickened.

**Symbiosis:** the living together of dissimilar organisms with benefit to both.

**Taxonomy:** the classification of plants or animals in systematic order.

**Terrestrial:** growing in the ground and supported by soil.

**Toothed:** with small triangular or rounded projections along the margin of the lip.

**Tuber:** a fleshy swollen underground stem or root formed annually; a food storage organ capable of producing new growth.

**Tuberculate:** covered with knobby projections.

**Undulate:** wavy.
**Unifoliate:** one-leaved.

**Variety:** a sub-division of a species differing from typical plants in a few unimportant characters; usually without special geographical distribution.

**Vein:** a thread of fibro-vascular tissue in a leaf or other organ.

**Viscidium:** a sticky disc connected to the pollinium, enabling it to adhere to an insect's body and to be carried away to another flower (19).

# CHECKLIST OF SPECIES OF THE ORCHIDS OF EUROPE, THE MIDDLE EAST AND NORTH AFRICA

| *Species* | *Locality* | *Date* |
|---|---|---|
| Lady's Slipper | | |
| *Cypripedium calceolus* (p. 24) | | |
| Rosy Lady's Slipper | | |
| *Cypripedium macranthum* (p. 26) | | |
| Spotted Lady's Slipper | | |
| *Cypripedium guttatum* (p. 28) | | |
| Cyprus Bee Orchid | | |
| *Ophrys kotschyi* (p. 30) | | |
| Cretan Bee Orchid | | |
| *Ophrys cretica* (p. 30) | | |
| Kurdish Bee Orchid | | |
| *Ophrys kurdica* (p. 30) | | |
| Reinhold's Bee Orchid | | |
| *Ophrys reinholdii* (p. 32) | | |
| Eyed Bee Orchid | | |
| *Ophrys argolica* (p. 32) | | |
| Crescent Ophrys | | |
| *Ophrys lunulata* (p. 34) | | |
| Luristan Ophrys | | |
| *Ophrys luristanica* (p. 34) | | |
| Mt Carmel Ophrys | | |
| *Ophrys carmelii* (p. 34) | | |
| Woodcock Orchid | | |
| *Ophrys scolopax* (pp. 34-6) | | |
| Late Spider Orchid | | |
| *Ophrys fuciflora* (pp. 38-42) | | |
| Sawfly Orchid | | |
| *Ophrys tenthredinifera* (p. 42) | | |
| Bee Orchid | | |
| *Ophrys apifera* (p. 44) | | |
| Bumble Bee Orchid | | |
| *Ophrys bombyliflora* (p. 46) | | |
| Horseshoe Orchid | | |
| *Ophrys ferrum-equinum* (p. 46) | | |
| Bertoloni's Bee Orchid | | |
| *Ophrys bertolonii* (p. 46) | | |
| Early Spider Orchid | | |
| *Ophrys sphegodes* (pp. 48-52) | | |
| Grecian Spider Orchid | | |
| *Ophrys spruneri* (p. 52) | | |
| False Spider Orchid | | |
| *Ophrys arachnitiformis* (p. 54) | | |
| Sombre Bee Orchid | | |
| *Ophrys fusca* (pp. 54-6) | | |
| Yellow Bee Orchid | | |
| *Ophrys lutea* (p. 56) | | |
| Pale Ophrys | | |
| *Ophrys pallida* (p. 58) | | |

| Species | Locality | Date |
|---------|----------|------|

Mirror Orchid
*Ophrys speculum* (p. 58).........................  ...........................................  ...............
Fly Orchid
*Ophrys insectifera* (p. 58).........................  ...........................................  ...............
Long-Lipped Serapias
*Serapias vomeracea* (p. 60).......................  ...........................................  ...............
Eastern Serapias
*Serapias orientalis* (p. 60) ........................  ...........................................  ...............
Scarce Serapias
*Serapias neglecta* (p. 62)...........................  ...........................................  ...............
Heart-Flowered Serapias
*Serapias cordigera* (p. 64) .........................  ...........................................  ...............
Small-Flowered Serapias
*Serapias parviflora* (p. 64) .......................  ...........................................  ...............
Hybrid Serapias
*Serapias olbia* (p. 66) .............................  ...........................................  ...............
Tongue Orchid
*Serapias lingua* (p. 66)............................  ...........................................  ...............
Man Orchid
*Aceras anthropophorum* (p. 66)...................  ...........................................  ...............
Lizard Orchid
*Himantoglossum hircinum* (pp. 68-72)..........  ...........................................  ...............
Short-Lobed Lizard Orchid
*Himantoglossum affine* (p. 74) ...................  ...........................................  ...............
Caucasian Lizard Orchid
*Himantoglossum formosum* (p. 76)..............  ...........................................  ...............
Giant Orchid
*Barlia robertiana* (p. 78) .........................  ...........................................  ...............
Pyramidal Orchid
*Anacamptis pyramidalis* (p. 80)..................  ...........................................  ...............
Dense-Flowered Orchid
*Neotinea maculata* (p. 80).......................  ...........................................  ...............
Bug Orchid
*Orchis coriophora* (p. 82).........................  ...........................................  ...............
Holy Orchid
*Orchis sancta* (p. 82) .............................  ...........................................  ...............
Burnt Orchid
*Orchis ustulata* (p. 84)...........................  ...........................................  ...............
Toothed Orchid
*Orchis tridentata* (p. 84)..........................  ...........................................  ...............
Milky Orchid
*Orchis lactea* (p. 84)..............................  ...........................................  ...............
Galilean Orchid
*Orchis galilaea* (p. 88) ...........................  ...........................................  ...............
Punctate Orchid
*Orchis punctulata* (p. 88)........................  ...........................................  ...............
Military Orchid
*Orchis militaris* (p. 88)...........................  ...........................................  ...............
Lady Orchid
*Orchis purpurea* (p. 88)...........................  ...........................................  ...............
Monkey Orchid
*Orchis simia* (p. 90)...............................  ...........................................  ...............

| Species | Locality | Date |
|---|---|---|

Naked Man Orchid
*Orchis italica* (p. 90) .............................. ........ .................... ..............

Green-winged Orchid
*Orchis morio* (p. 92) .............................. ........................................ ..............

Pink Butterfly Orchid
*Orchis papilionacea* (p. 94) ...................... ........................................ ..............

Long-Spurred Orchid
*Orchis longicornu* (p. 94) ........................ ........................................ ..............

Fan-Lipped Orchid
*Orchis saccata* (p. 96) ............................ ........................................ ..............

Green-Spotted Orchid
*Orchis patens* (p. 96) ............................. ........................................ ..............

Spitzel's Orchid
*Orchis spitzelii* (p. 96) . ......................... ........................................ ..............

Canary Islands Orchid
*Orchis canariensis* (p. 98) ........................ ........................................ ..............

Anatolian Orchid
*Orchis anatolica* (p. 98) .......................... ........................................ ..............

Four-Spotted Orchid
*Orchis quadripunctata* (p. 98) ................... ........................................ ..............

Bory's Orchid
*Orchis boryi* (p. 98) ............................... ........................................ ..............

Early Purple Orchid
*Orchis mascula* (p. 100) .......................... ........................................ ..............

Pale-Flowered Orchid
*Orchis pallens* (p. 102) ........................... ........................................ ..............

Provence Orchid
*Orchis provincialis* (p. 102) ..................... ........................................ ..............

Loose-Flowered Orchid
*Orchis laxiflora* (p. 104) ......................... ........................................ ..............

Komper's Orchid
*Comperia comperiana* (p. 106) .................. ........................................ ..............

Hooded Orchid
*Steveniella satyrioides* (p. 106) ................. ........................................ ..............

Crimean Orchid
*Dactylorhiza iberica* (p. 108) ................... ........................................ ..............

Elder-Flowered Orchid
*Dactylorhiza sambucina* (p. 108) ............... ........................................ ..............

Roman Orchid
*Dactylorhiza romana* (p. 108) ................... ........................................ ..............

Early Marsh Orchid
*Dactylorhiza incarnata* (p. 110) ................ ........................................ ..............

Robust Marsh Orchid
*Dactylorhiza elata* (p. 112) ...................... ........................................ ..............

Broad-Leaved Marsh Orchid
*Dactylorhiza majalis* (p. 112) ................... ........................................ ..............

Southern Marsh Orchid
*Dactylorhiza praetermissa* (p. 114) ............ ........................................ ..............

Northern Marsh Orchid
*Dactylorhiza purpurella* (p. 114) ............... ........................................ ..............

Scandinavian Marsh Orchid
*Dactylorhiza pseudocordigera* (p. 114) ........ ........................................ ..............

| *Species* | *Locality* | *Date* |
|---|---|---|

Heart-Shaped Orchid
*Dactylorhiza cordigera* (p. 116).................    ............................................    ...............

Pugsley's Marsh Orchid
*Dactylorhiza traunsteineri* (p. 116)..............    ............................................    ...............

Anatolian Marsh Orchid
*Dactylorhiza cilicica* (p. 116)....................    ............................................    ...............

Madeiran Orchid
*Dactylorhiza foliosa* (p. 118).....................    ............................................    ...............

Wedge-Lipped Orchid
*Dactylorhiza saccifera* (p. 118).................    ............................................    ...............

Caucasian Marsh Orchid
*Dactylorhiza cataonica* (p. 118).................    ............................................    ...............

Lapland Marsh Orchid
*Dactylorhiza lapponica* (p. 120).................    ............................................    ...............

Common Spotted Orchid
*Dactylorhiza fuchsii* (p. 120).....................    ............................................    ...............

Heath Spotted Orchid
*Dactylorhiza maculata* (p. 120).................    ............................................    ...............

Globe Orchid
*Traunsteinera globosa* (p. 122)...................    ............................................    ...............

Dwarf Alpine Orchid
*Chamorchis alpina* (p. 122) .....................    ............................................    ...............

Black Vanilla Orchid
*Nigritella nigra* (p. 122)...........................    ............................................    ...............

Fragrant Orchid
*Gymnadenia conopsea* (p. 124) .................    ............................................    ...............

Short-Spurred Fragrant Orchid
*Gymnadenia odoratissima* (p. 124)..............    ............................................    ...............

Small White Orchid
*Leucorchis albida* (p. 126)........................    ............................................    ...............

Frivald's Frog Orchid
*Leucorchis frivaldii* (p. 126)....................    ............................................    ...............

Pink Frog Orchid
*Neottianthe cucullata* (p. 126)...................    ............................................    ...............

Frog Orchid
*Coeloglossum viride* (p. 126)....................    ............................................    ...............

Lesser Butterfly Orchid
*Platanthera bifolia* (p. 128).....................    ............................................    ...............

Greater Butterfly Orchid
*Platanthera chlorantha* (p. 128)................    ............................................    ...............

Azores Butterfly Orchid
*Platanthera micrantha* (p. 128)................    ............................................    ...............

Algerian Butterfly Orchid
*Platanthera algeriensis* (p. 130)................    ............................................    ...............

One-Leaved Butterfly Orchid
*Platanthera obtusata* (p. 130)....................    ............................................    ...............

Northern Butterfly Orchid
*Platanthera hyperborea* (p. 130) ................    ............................................    ...............

Three-Lobed Habenaria
*Habenaria tridactylites* (p. 132)................    ............................................    ...............

Two-Leaved Scrub Orchid
*Gennaria diphylla* (p. 132)........................    ............................................    ...............

| Species | Locality | Date |
|---------|----------|------|

Musk Orchid
*Herminium monorchis* (p. 132)............... ........................................... ...............
Fen Orchid
*Liparis loeselii* (p. 134)....................... ........................................... ...............
Calypso
*Calypso bulbosa* (p. 134)..................... ........................................... ...............
Coralroot
*Corallorhiza trifida* (p. 134)............... ........................................... ...............
Bog Orchid
*Hammarbya paludosa* (p. 136).............. ........................................... ...............
Single-Leaved Bog Orchid
*Malaxis monophyllos* (p. 136).............. ........................................... ...............
Creeping Lady's Tresses
*Goodyera repens* (p. 136)................... ........................................... ...............
Madeiran Lady's Tresses
*Goodyera macrophylla* (p. 138)............ ........................................... ...............
Autumn Lady's Tresses
*Spiranthes spiralis* (p. 138)............... ........................................... ...............
Pink Lady's Tresses
*Spiranthes sinensis* (p. 138).............. ........................................... ...............
Summer Lady's Tresses
*Spiranthes aestivalis* (p. 138)............ ........................................... ...............
Irish Lady's Tresses
*Spiranthes romanzoffiana* (p. 138)....... ........................................... ...............
Bird's Nest Orchid
*Neottia nidus-avis* (p. 140)............... ........................................... ...............
Common Twayblade
*Listera ovata* (p. 140)...................... ........................................... ...............
Lesser Twayblade
*Listera cordata* (p. 140)................... ........................................... ...............
Spurred Coralroot
*Epipogium aphyllum* (p. 142).............. ........................................... ...............
Violet Limodore
*Limodorum abortivum* (p. 142)........... ........................................... ...............
Large White Helleborine
*Cephalanthera damasonium* (p. 144)...... ........................................... ...............
Sword-Leaved Helleborine
*Cephalanthera longifolia* (p. 144)........ ........................................... ...............
Red Helleborine
*Cephalanthera rubra* (p. 146)............. ........................................... ...............
Hooded Helleborine
*Cephalanthera cucullata* (p. 146).......... ........................................... ...............
Eastern Hooded Helleborine
*Cephalanthera epipactoides* (p. 146)...... ........................................... ...............
Marsh Helleborine
*Epipactis palustris* (p. 148)............... ........................................... ...............
Scarce Marsh Helleborine
*Epipactis veratrifolia* (p. 148)............ ........................................... ...............
Broad-Leaved Helleborine
*Epipactis helleborine* (p. 150)............. ........................................... ...............
Cyprus Helleborine
*Epipactis troodii* (p. 150)................. ........................................... ...............

| *Species* | *Locality* | *Date* |
|---|---|---|
| Violet Helleborine | | |
| *Epipactis purpurata* (p. 152)..................... | ........................................... | .............. |
| Eastern Violet Helleborine | | |
| *Epipactis condensata* (p. 152)................... | ........................................... | .............. |
| Mueller's Helleborine | | |
| *Epipactis muelleri* (p. 152)........................ | ........................................... | .............. |
| Pendulous-Flowered Helleborine | | |
| *Epipactis phyllanthes* (p. 154)................... | ........................................... | .............. |
| Pontus Helleborine | | |
| *Epipactis pontica* (p. 154)........................ | ........................................... | .............. |
| Persian Helleborine | | |
| *Epipactis persica* (p. 156)........................ | ........................................... | .............. |
| Narrow-Lipped Helleborine | | |
| *Epipactis leptochila* (p. 156)..................... | ........................................... | .............. |
| Dune Helleborine | | |
| *Epipactis dunensis* (p. 156)...................... | ........................................... | .............. |
| Dark Red Helleborine | | |
| *Epipactis atrorubens* (p. 158)..................... | ........................................... | .............. |
| Small-Leaved Helleborine | | |
| *Epipactis microphylla* (p. 158)................... | ........................................... | .............. |

# INDEX

*NB Subspecies are indexed only where the*
*species extends over more than one page.*